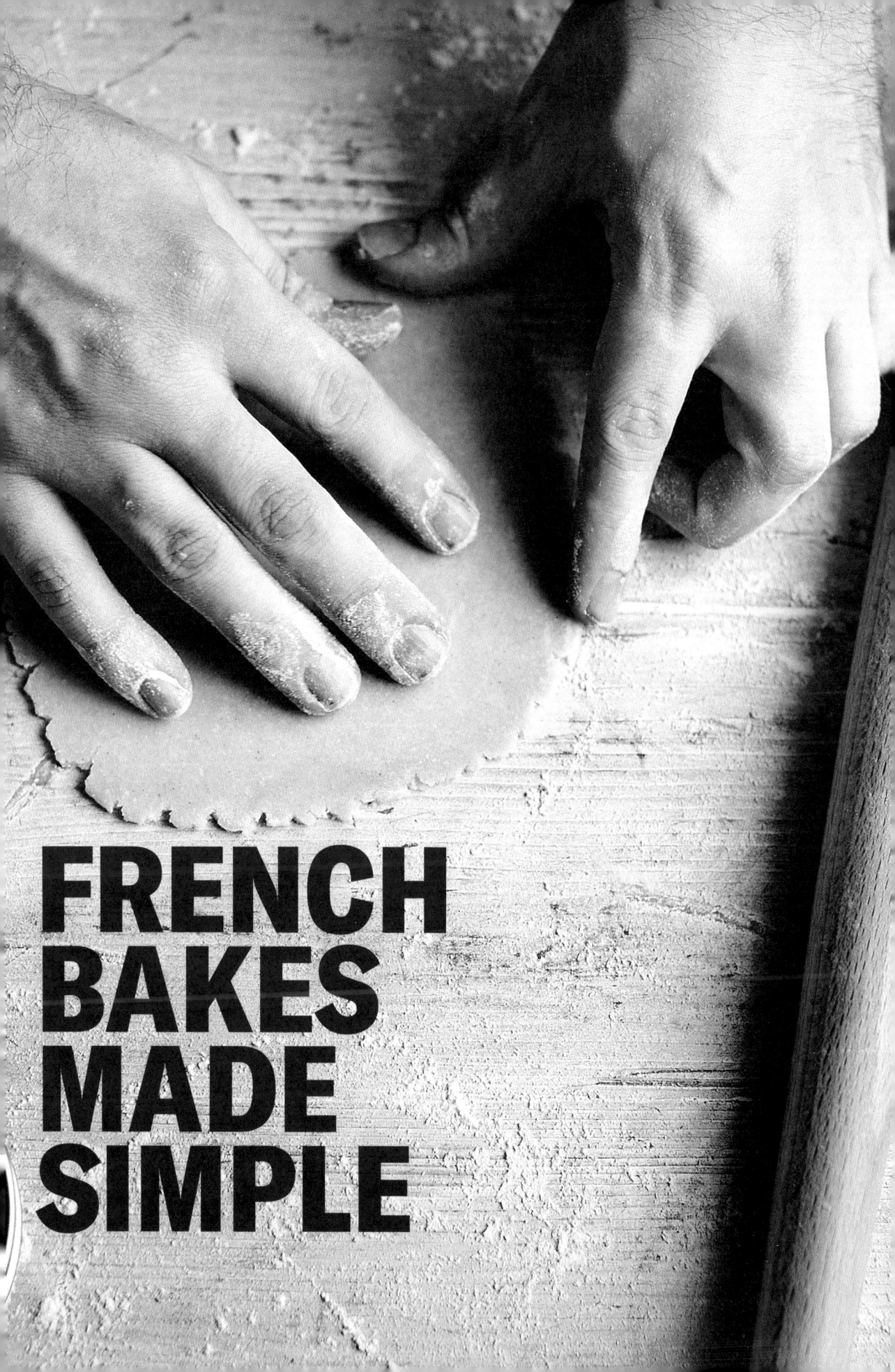

FRENCH BAKES MADE SIMPLE

TO SIMON, NICOLA AND NEIL

FRENCH BAKES MADE SIMPLE

From macaron to millefeuille and more

Edd Kimber

PHOTOGRAPHY BY LAURA EDWARDS

Edd Kimber is a baker, food writer and TV personality. He fought off competition from 4,000 applicants to become the first winner of *The Great British Bake Off* on BBC2. Since then Edd has appeared on many TV shows including *Sunday Brunch* and *The Alan Titchmarsh Show* as well his own show on Food Network UK *John and Edd's Christmas Bakes*. Edd's recipes are regularly featured in magazines such as *BBC Good Food Magazine*, *Olive* and *Waitrose Weekend* and he has also appeared in numerous national newspapers including the *Independent* and the *Sun*. He is a regular at food festivals across the country including the BBC Good Food Show Live. Edd is the author of several cookbooks, including: *One Tin Bakes, One Tin Bakes Easy, Small Batch Bakes* and *Small Batch Cookies*. www.theboywhobakes.co.uk

'Edd's desserts taste as good as they look...these delicious recipes inspire the baker in all of us.' Philippe Conticini

K
KYLE
BOOKS

Contents

Introduction **6**

Pastry **12**

Cakes & desserts **50**

Sweet treats **92**

Masterclass **128**

Basics **154**

Resources **188**   Index **189**

Introduction

I've had a love affair with France since I was a small boy, after spending many very happy holidays in Bordeaux and Brittany. I have memories of stopping by the side of the road after my parents had driven through the night to enjoy a simple breakfast of croissants and jam, or using my rather rusty primary-school French to try to buy some canelés in Saint-Émilion. I'm sure I only succeeded because that was all the shop sold!

Many of my memories of France are intertwined with memories of food: the time the owner of a wine shop allowed my brother and me to join in with a wine tasting, even though we were far too young, or the trip where every morning we would walk to the bakery for a pain au chocolat fresh from the oven. For me, France is Food.

The first time I truly fell in love with France was while I was studying at university in Lancaster. It was my first term and my first student loan had just been cashed. With the money burning a hole in my pocket, three friends and I decided, on a whim, that we really needed to visit Paris. We stayed in a dingy hotel miles from anything, but we had the best time. Within hours of arriving we were sitting across from the Eiffel Tower as it started its nightly light show, enjoying the cheapest bottle of wine we could buy, accompanied with what I remember as copious amounts of cheese. But what made me fall in love with French baking was stumbling across Pierre Hermé's Saint-Germain boutique. I had been baking since I was little, but it was always very homely, humble recipes that I had grown up with. I had never seen the art that pastry could be, so refined and beautiful. This was also the first time I tried a macaron, which became an obsession and is a recipe I credit with making me think I could make a living out of baking. Shortly after this trip, I decided that even though I might not make much money I would try to make a career out of my passion for baking – what better way than to make a living doing what you love!

Over the years, I have visited France on a regular basis, at least once or twice a year, eating my way around the country: salted caramels in Brittany, kougelhopf in Alsace and tarte Tropezienne in Saint-Tropez. In this book I want to take you on a tour of France and pass on the love I have for this country and its delicious recipes. Some of the recipes are classic and traditional, some are my interpretation of an idea and some are inspired by the modern influence that can be seen on the counters of pâtisseries around France. Above all, the recipes are all achievable in the home kitchen. This is not meant to be a professional pâtisserie book that will sit on your shelf and never be used. I want you in the kitchen, making beautiful cakes and sharing them with your friends and family.

I have, where possible, avoided using equipment that is either hard to get hold of or a speciality item that you might only ever use once or twice. There are a couple of exceptions to this rule, but only because the alternative makes an inferior result. I have also tried to use widely available ingredients with only a few that are not available in supermarkets, although they can be purchased online (see Resources, page 188).

After reading and baking your way through this book, I hope you will fall for France as I have, and I also hope that one day you will visit there, if you haven't already, and enjoy some of the best baking in the world.

Bon appetit!

Edd Kimber

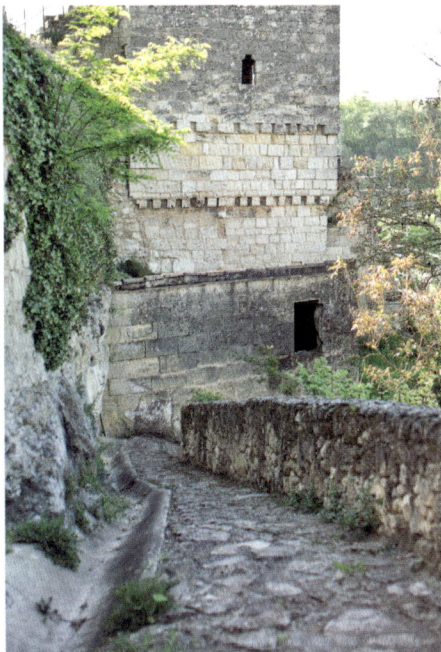

Equipment

This book is aimed at people like you and me – home bakers – so I have tried, where possible, to use equipment that is easy to get hold of and that you may already have in your cupboards at home. Where I have suggested specialized equipment, I have endeavoured to give an alternative because, most of all, I want these recipes to be baked and enjoyed.

TART RINGS AND TINS

For the recipes in this book I have used tart rings 8cm (3¼in) and 23cm (9in) in diameter, but in most recipes these can be replaced with equivalent loose-based tart tins. These have fluted edges, so the look will be a little different but they will taste the same.

CAKE RINGS

Some of the mousses and cakes are assembled inside a cake ring – a simple ring of metal used to help construct cakes. Although you can buy these from any good kitchen shop, you can also use the ring from a springform cake tin with no problem.

BAKING MOULDS

This book has a few recipes that use specialized moulds, including the madeleines and the canelés. Generally, I prefer metal versions of these moulds, but there are also silicone versions available, which are generally cheaper and which I would recommend if you won't be baking the recipe often. The only exception to this is the canelés, which I would always suggest baking in the traditional copper moulds. You can, of course, use a silicone mould, making sure you buy high quality, but I have never been able to get quite as good a finish as when I use the copper. As with all bakeware, when buying silicone, make sure to buy good quality; if the mould seems cheap and flimsy, it is best avoided. Look for sturdy versions with well-defined shapes.

SMALL EQUIPMENT

You don't need a kitchen full of equipment, but the basics are the key to good baking. These include heatproof spatulas, balloon whisks in different sizes, wooden spoons, a microplane zester, a large rolling pin, a set of round cookie cutters and my all-time favourite piece of equipment: the offset spatula (in small and large), which I guarantee you will end up using very often.

BAKING TRAYS

I prefer to use sheet pans instead of flat baking trays as the rim of a sheet pan makes it much more useful. You can use it to catch drips when glazing a cake, or bake the layers of joconde for the Gâteau Opéra (page 132). My favourite supplier of these is Nordic Ware.

BOWLS

There is no getting away from it, baking uses a lot of bowls, so it is good to have a supply of them on hand. My preference is for Pyrex bowls, as they are available in a large array of sizes and are extremely durable as well as being heatproof.

BLOWTORCH

A great kitchen tool, I would definitely recommend you purchase a kitchen blowtorch, because they are perfect for caramelizing a crème brûlée or to help loosen a frozen mousse from its mould. But if you don't have one, you can use alternatives. Crème brûlées can be caramelized under the grill and a tea towel that has been soaked in hot water and wrung out can be used to help loosen frozen desserts.

SCALES

This is something I am a bit evangelical about. A cheap set of electric scales will instantly improve your baking. Baking by volume is inherently inaccurate and old-fashioned spring-style scales lose accuracy over time. I implore you to spend a very small amount of money to make a big difference to your baking.

THERMOMETER

When making temperature-specific recipes, such as caramels or even custards, I find an instant-read thermometer an invaluable tool. My personal favourite is the Thermapen, a good investment if you're a passionate baker and cook. If you want a cheaper alternative, an old-fashioned sugar thermometer will do the job for most things, but look after it very carefully as they are prone to damage (or that might just be my heavy-handedness).

PIPING BAGS AND TIPS

I use a lot of piping bags, it helps to give a polished finish to recipes, but I don't like the old-fashioned nylon bags – they're fiddly to wash up, and my inner messy baker loves disposable bags. You can buy small versions from supermarkets, but they tend to be too small and poor quality; however, any good kitchen store will sell high-quality ones (see Resources, page 188). I only use a small amount of piping tips, a few different-sized round tips, a St Honoré tip and a few different-sized star tips.

FREESTANDING ELECTRIC MIXER

You don't need an electric mixer to bake, but some recipes are much easier when using one; brioche, for example, is much less daunting when the machine can do the work for you. If you love to bake, then trust me when I say you will never regret buying a mixer – they are an invaluable tool. If you don't want to spend as much money, a high-quality hand mixer will do a good job for most recipes.

UK/US GLOSSARY OF TERMS

Baking parchment	Baking paper
Baking tray	Baking sheet
Bicarbonate of soda	Baking soda
Caster sugar	Superfine sugar
Clingfilm	Plastic wrap
Cornflour	Cornstarch
Desiccated coconut	Dried shredded coconut
Double cream	Heavy cream
Flaked almonds	Slivered almonds
Frying pan	Skillet
Golden syrup	Light corn syrup
Grill	Broiler
Ground almonds	Almond meal
Hob	Stovetop
Icing sugar	Confectioners' sugar
Kitchen paper	Paper towels
Plain flour	All-purpose flour
Self-raising flour	Self-rising flour
Semi-skimmed milk	Low-fat milk
Tea towel	Cloth kitchen towel
Tin	Pan
Vanilla pod	Vanilla bean

Ingredients

French baking often relies on just one or two flavours, letting the beauty of those products shine. Therefore it is important to use good-quality ingredients where possible.

CHOCOLATE

The world of chocolate is one that is wonderful and endlessly varied. I could happily write another book on that subject alone, but as a general rule, try to use high-quality chocolate that doesn't include too many ingredients. Check the packet, and if it includes a long list of ingredients that you don't recognize or understand, it might be best avoided. Good-quality chocolate should really only include cocoa solids, cocoa butter, sugar and possibly vanilla and soya lecithin, but if it has anything else, it might not be high enough in quality. Although I have listed a suggested cocoa solid content for the chocolate for each recipe, these are only a guide. Unless you are making a ganache, changing to a chocolate with a different cocoa solid percentage won't affect the recipe too much; it is much more important to use a chocolate that you enjoy the flavour of. The recipes in this book were tested with a variety of chocolates including Green & Black's, Valrhona, Amedei and Cacao Barry.

BUTTER

All the recipes in this book were tested with butter that has a high butter-fat content, at least 84 per cent, which in Europe is the standard. If making these recipes in the US, look for European-style high butter-fat-style butters. As butter often adds lots of flavour, try to use the best quality you can afford. It really can make a difference. Although it is very common to use salted butter for baking in France, I have always preferred to use unsalted, adding the salt myself, but if all you have is salted there is no problem with it, simply cut back on or eliminate the salt in the recipe.

SUGAR

Visiting French supermarkets I found that generally it was harder to find muscovado or light brown sugars, so I have kept their use to a minimum, but of course where I have listed caster sugar I would happily encourage you to use a golden unrefined variety, which has wonderful caramel notes. The exception to this would be when making sugar syrups where this flavour isn't always desired.

SALT

The French are famous for their wonderful varieties of salt, including fleur de sel, but if that is not available, use whatever good-quality flaked sea salt you can find, such as Maldon or Halen Môn, a Welsh sea salt I'm very partial to. The only time I use fine salt is in recipes such as brioche and croissant dough where I want the salt to blend into the dough a little easier than flaked salt does.

FRUIT

Where possible I would always suggest using fruit that is in season for the simple reason that it tastes a lot better. Anyone who has tasted out-of-season strawberries will understand what I'm talking about. There are times, however, when frozen fruit can be used. Recipes such as the Cassis Religieuse (page 37), where the fruit is being turned into a purée, is a perfect candidate for using frozen fruit, and in the same manner, frozen fruit purées can often be a lifesaver. I have a soft spot for passion fruit, and use it a lot, so if you can find frozen passion fruit purée, it is a great ingredient to stash away in your freezer, and it is also a lot cheaper than buying the individual fruits.

CREAM

For this book I have generally used whipping cream, which has a fat content of 35 per cent and is comparable to French crème liquide and American heavy cream. It has a lighter taste than double cream, which has a 48 per cent fat content and is better suited to pâtisserie.

EGGS

Unless stated otherwise, all eggs in this book are large and my preference is to use free-range organic eggs.

VANILLA

I absolutely love the aroma and flavour of real vanilla pods and prefer to use the Madagascan variety (for flavour and price). Although Tahitian pods have a wonderful flavour, they tend to be more expensive, and Madagascan pods have the classic flavour most people associate with vanilla. If you don't have vanilla pods, a great alternative is vanilla bean paste, which is a thick sugar syrup packed full of vanilla seeds and much cheaper than the pods themselves. As a guide, I find 2 teaspoons of paste is equivalent to 1 vanilla pod.

CHAPTER ONE

PASTRY

Raspberry Tarts

The raspberry tart is a recipe that screams summer, a timeless classic that is a staple in all bakeries. As with any recipe using berries, it really is best made when raspberries are in season – that way this simple tart will be more than the sum of its parts. If you want to enhance the flavour in this recipe, you could add chocolate to the crème pâtissière or even a touch of orange or lemon zest. Personally, I like it exactly as it is – sometimes simple is best.

MAKES 6

½ recipe Pâte Sucrée
  (see page 158), chilled
½ recipe Crème Pâtissière
  (see page 178), chilled
300g (10½oz) raspberries
icing sugar or seedless raspberry jam,
  to decorate

Preheat the oven to 180°C (160°C fan/350°F), Gas Mark 4 and line a baking tray with baking parchment. To make the tart shells, line individual tart rings or tart tins with the pastry according to the instructions on page 164. Set the pastry shells onto the prepared baking tray and put it in the refrigerator to chill for 30 minutes or until the pastry is firm.

Line the tarts with baking parchment and fill with baking beans or rice. Bake for 15 minutes, then remove the parchment and the baking beans and bake for a further 10 minutes or until the pastry is golden. Set aside and leave to cool.

Remove the crème pâtissière from the refrigerator and beat it with a spatula to loosen. Divide between the tart shells and top with the raspberries. To finish, you can either simply dust with a little icing sugar or heat some seedless raspberry jam until bubbling and use this to glaze the raspberries.

All the elements can be prepared in advance, but once assembled the tarts are best served on the day they are made.

Lemon Tart

It is often said that the mark of a good pâtisserie or restaurant is the quality of its lemon tart – a deceptively simple recipe – and I would agree. Although the basic recipe is fairly straightforward – a lemon custard baked in a sweet pastry shell – making a perfect example with the right textures and flavours is the sign of a great pastry chef. My version isn't a classic baked tart but a slightly more modern and easier take on the classic, using a lemon cream.

SERVES 12

½ recipe Pâte Sucrée
   (see page 158), chilled
flour for dusting

FOR THE LEMON CREAM
150ml (¼ pint) lemon juice
2 large eggs
2 large egg yolks
150g (5½oz) caster sugar
225g (8oz) unsalted butter, diced
   and chilled

FOR THE DECORATION
icing sugar
a few pistachio nuts, finely chopped
   (optional)

Preheat the oven to 180°C (160°C fan/350°F), Gas Mark 4 and line a baking tray with baking parchment. Roll out the pastry on a lightly floured work surface until it is about 2–3mm (¹⁄₁₆–⅛in) thick. Use this to line a 23cm (9in) tart ring or loose-based tart tin set onto your prepared baking tray. Trim off the excess pastry and put the tart in the refrigerator for 30 minutes or until firm.

Line the tart shell with a layer of baking parchment and fill with baking beans or rice. Bake for 25 minutes, then remove the parchment and the beans and bake for a further 10 minutes or until the pastry is golden. Remove from the oven and leave to cool completely before assembling.

To make the lemon cream, put the lemon juice, eggs, yolks and sugar in a large pan over a medium heat. Stir the mixture constantly, until it reaches 75–80°C (167–176°F) on an instant-read thermometer. (If you are worried about curdling the mixture, you can cook this in a heatproof bowl set over a pan of gently simmering water, but it will take longer.)

Pour the lemon mixture through a fine sieve into a medium bowl and leave to cool for 15 minutes or until lukewarm. Add the butter a few pieces at a time and, using a hand blender, process until smooth. Press a piece of clingfilm onto the surface of the cream and put it in the refrigerator for a few hours, or preferably overnight, until completely set.

Once the cream has set, stir lightly to loosen, then spread it onto the base of the tart, smoothing it into an even layer. Put the tart into the refrigerator and leave to chill for 2 hours before serving.

To decorate, put a little icing sugar in a sieve and use to dust over the edge of the tart, then sprinkle the pistachio nuts around the outside of the tart, if you like.

This tart will keep for up to three days in the refrigerator.

Chocolate Soufflé Tarts with Salted Caramel

Being totally honest, this isn't a classic French recipe, it is, however, inspired by two very French ideas – chocolate mousse and salted caramel – and it uses them to create one of my all-time favourite recipes. Rather innocent looking, these tarts are filled with a layer of liquid salted caramel and topped with a layer of chocolate mousse that is baked, so that when you cut into the tart you get a light-as-a-feather chocolate cake with a liquid caramel filling.

MAKES 6

½ recipe Pâte Sucrée (see page 158)
  or Sweet Chocolate Pastry
  (see page 158), chilled

FOR THE SALTED CARAMEL FILLING

130g (4½oz) caster sugar
pinch of flaked sea salt
130ml (4fl oz) double cream
20g (¾oz) unsalted butter

FOR THE CHOCOLATE SOUFFLÉ TOPPING

75g (2½oz) unsalted butter
100g (3½oz) dark chocolate (70 per cent
  cocoa solids), finely chopped
2 large eggs, separated
75g (2½oz) caster sugar

TIP

You can prepare the caramel two days in advance, but reheat it slightly in a pan over a low heat to make it easier to pour.

Line a baking tray with baking parchment. To make the salted caramel, put the caster sugar in a small pan over a medium heat and leave, without stirring, until it has dissolved and turned a golden brown. Be careful that it doesn't cook too far as it can burn easily.

Meanwhile, put the salt, cream and butter in a small pan over a medium heat and heat until just below boiling. Once the sugar has caramelized, carefully pour half the cream mixture into the caramel, still on the heat. Once the bubbling has subsided, pour in the remaining cream and stir to combine. Pour the caramel into a heatproof jug and set aside.

Using the instructions on page 164, line six individual tart rings or tart tins with the pâte sucrée, then put them on the prepared baking tray and transfer them to the refrigerator to chill for 30 minutes or until firm. Preheat the oven to 180°C (160°C fan/350°F), Gas Mark 4.

Line each tart with baking parchment and fill with baking beans or rice. Bake for 15 minutes, then remove the baking beans and parchment, and return to the oven for another 5 minutes.

Divide the caramel between the tarts and leave to cool to room temperature, then chill in the refrigerator while you make the topping.

To make the chocolate soufflé, put the butter and chocolate in a large, heatproof bowl set over a pan of gently simmering water, making sure the base of the bowl doesn't touch the water. Stir the chocolate occasionally until fully melted. Remove from the heat and leave to cool slightly. In a separate bowl, whisk the egg yolks with 50g (1¾oz) of the sugar until thick and pale. Whisk this into the slightly cooled chocolate mixture.

Put the egg whites into a clean, grease-free bowl and, using an electric mixer, whisk until they form soft peaks. Continue to whisk while you slowly pour in the remaining sugar until the meringue is stiff and glossy. In three additions, fold the meringue into the chocolate mixture.

To assemble, remove the tarts from the refrigerator and top with the mousse mixture. Bake for 15 minutes or until the mousse looks set. Allow to cool a little before serving slightly warm or, if you prefer, at room temperature. The tarts will keep for up to two days but are best reheated in the oven at 120°C (100°C fan/250°F), Gas Mark ½ for 10 minutes.

Passion Fruit and Chocolate Tart

The combination of passion fruit and chocolate might seem unusual, but it has become a modern French classic, seen in many pâtisseries and used in everything from macarons to elegant cakes. It is also one of my favourite combinations, one that always keeps me coming back for more. Instead of a curd, it uses a passion fruit cream, very similar to a curd recipe but with more butter so that when it is cold it sets firmer, allowing it to hold the weight of the chocolate topping.

SERVES 12

flour for dusting
Sweet Chocolate Pastry (see page 158), chilled
approx. 2 teaspoons cocoa powder, to decorate

FOR THE PASSION FRUIT CREAM
75ml (2½fl oz) passion fruit purée (approx. 5 passion fruit)
1 large egg
1 large egg yolk
50g (1¾oz) caster sugar
115g (4oz) unsalted butter, diced and slightly softened

FOR THE GANACHE
150ml (¼ pint) whipping cream
15g (½oz) unsalted butter
100g (3½oz) milk chocolate (30–40 per cent cocoa solids), finely chopped
50g (1¾oz) dark chocolate (60–70 per cent cocoa solids), finely chopped

Preheat the oven to 180°C (160°C fan/350°F), Gas Mark 4 and line a baking tray with baking parchment. Roll out the pastry on a lightly floured work surface and line a 23cm (9in) loose-based tart tin or tart ring according to the instructions on page 164. Line the pastry with a layer of baking parchment and fill the tart with baking beans or rice. Bake for 25 minutes, then remove the baking beans and parchment and bake for a further 10 minutes or until crisp.

To make the passion fruit purée, halve the passion fruit and scrape out the seeds and flesh into a sieve set over a small bowl. Push the flesh and juice through the sieve and measure out 75ml (2½fl oz) of this purée. To make the passion fruit cream, put the purée, egg, yolk and sugar in a medium pan over a medium heat. Stir the mixture constantly, until it reaches 75–80°C (167–176°F) on an instant-read thermometer. Pour the passion fruit mixture through a fine sieve into a medium bowl and leave to cool for 15 minutes or until lukewarm. Add the butter a few pieces at a time and, using a hand blender, process until smooth. Press a piece of clingfilm onto the surface of the cream and transfer it to the refrigerator for a few hours, or preferably overnight, until completely set.

Stir the passion fruit mixture lightly to loosen it, then spread it into the base of the tart, filling it halfway and reserving a few tablespoons of the mixture. Transfer the tart to the refrigerator and leave to chill for 2 hours.

To make the ganache, put the cream and butter in a small pan and bring to the boil. Put both types of chocolate in a medium bowl and, once the cream is just boiling, pour it over the chocolate and leave for a few minutes, then stir, to form a smooth, shiny ganache. Leave the ganache to cool for a few minutes before pouring it onto the chilled tart and gently spreading it to cover the surface. At this point it is preferable to keep the tart out of the refrigerator, as the texture of the ganache is much silkier this way; however, if you are not serving the tart on the day it is assembled, keep it in the refrigerator but remove it a few hours before serving.

To decorate the tart, sieve the cocoa powder over the tart. Beat the reserved passion fruit cream to loosen it. Put it into a disposable piping bag and snip off the end. Pipe a number of different-sized rounds on top of the cocoa powder. This tart is best eaten on the day it is assembled, but you can make the pastry the day before and the cream up to a week in advance.

Pear Tart

Tarts like this originate from the north-east of France in Alsace. Home to delicious rustic bakes such as the Kougelhopf (page 108) and the tarte fine aux pommes, the poached pear tart is another straightforward but delectable recipe. The pears are gently poached in a syrup flavoured with lemon giving the finished tart a simple but vibrant flavour – perfect if you are looking for something that isn't too sweet or filling.

SERVES 10

FOR THE FRANGIPANE
100g (3½oz) unsalted butter, at
   room temperature
100g (3½oz) caster sugar
2 large eggs
100g (3½oz) ground almonds

FOR THE POACHED PEARS
150g (5½oz) caster sugar
1 lemon
2 Conference or Bosc pears

FOR THE PASTRY
½ recipe Pâte Sucrée (see page 158) or
   Pâte Brisée (see page 160), chilled
flour, for dusting

FOR THE DECORATION
2 tablespoons flaked almonds
2 tablespoons clear apricot jam

To make the frangipane, put the butter and sugar in a bowl and, using an electric mixer, beat together for 5 minutes or until light and fluffy. Add the eggs one at a time, beating until fully combined before adding the next. Add the ground almonds and mix to combine. Set aside until needed. If you want to prepare this ahead, the frangipane can be made two days in advance, just cover and chill until needed (bring to room temperature before using).

To poach the pears, put 500ml (18fl oz) water and the caster sugar in a medium pan. Using a sharp knife, cut off three strips of lemon zest and add to the pan. Bring the mixture to a gentle simmer over a medium heat. Squeeze the juice from the lemon into a bowl and set aside. Peel, halve and core the pears, putting them into the bowl of lemon juice as you work to prevent the fruit from browning. Add the pears and lemon juice to the syrup and poach for 15–20 minutes or until tender. Remove the pan from the heat and set aside while you prepare the tart.

To make the tart, roll out the pastry on a lightly floured work surface into a rectangle about 2–3mm (¹⁄₁₆–⅛in) thick. Use to line a 35 × 11cm (14 × 4¼in) loose-based tart tin (see page 164 for how to line a tart tin). Transfer the tart shell to the refrigerator for 30 minutes or until firm. Preheat the oven to 180°C (160°C fan/350°F), Gas Mark 4.

Line the pastry with a sheet of baking parchment and fill it with baking beans or rice. Bake for 20 minutes, then remove the parchment and baking beans and bake for a further 5 minutes or until the base is a pale golden colour. Remove from the oven and leave to cool for 5 minutes.

To assemble the tart, fill with the frangipane, spreading it into an even layer. Press the pears into the frangipane, cut-side down, and sprinkle the tart with the flaked almonds. Bake for 25–30 minutes until the frangipane is golden. Remove from the oven and leave to cool in the tin. While cooling, put the apricot jam in a small pan and bring to the boil, then remove from the heat and, while still hot, brush over the tart.

The tart is best served the day it is made, but it will still be good the day after. Any longer and the pastry will start to soften.

Coffee Tart

The French love coffee, but until recently I had always found it difficult to get a decent cup. They even refer to their coffee as 'jus de chaussette' – sock juice! Over recent years it has become much easier to find the good stuff. In Paris, especially, there is so much more quality available. Coffee is also one of the classic pastry flavours. Everything from éclairs to cakes come in this basic flavour, alongside chocolate, vanilla and pistachio. Here is my version of this classic; it's meant to remind you of a cappuccino, but it also tastes similar to tiramisu.

SERVES 12

Sweet Chocolate Pastry
 (see page 158), chilled
flour, for dusting
cocoa powder, for dusting

FOR THE BISCUIT À LA CUILLÈRE

2 large eggs, separated
35g (1¼oz) caster sugar
50g (1¾oz) plain flour
6 tablespoons very strong black coffee

FOR THE COFFEE AND WHITE CHOCOLATE GANACHE

125ml (4fl oz) whipping cream
1 tablespoon finely ground coffee
250g (9oz) white chocolate,
 finely chopped

FOR THE MASCARPONE CREAM

150g (5½oz) mascarpone
200ml (7fl oz) whipping cream
1 tablespoon icing sugar

TIP
If you want to skip the sponge filling, you can use some store-bought sponge fingers instead.

Preheat the oven to 180°C (160°C fan/350°F), Gas Mark 4 and line a baking tray with baking parchment. Roll out the pastry on a lightly floured work surface and line a 23cm (9in) loose-based tart tin or tart ring according to the instructions on page 164. Line the pastry with a layer of baking parchment and fill the tart with baking beans or rice. Bake for 25 minutes, then remove the baking beans and parchment and bake for a further 10 minutes or until crisp.

To make the biscuit à la cuillère, reduce the oven temperature to 160°C (140°C fan/325°F), Gas Mark 3. Put the egg whites in a clean, grease-free bowl and, using an electric mixer, whisk until they form stiff peaks. Continue whisking and slowly pour in the sugar until the mixture becomes stiff and glossy.

In a separate bowl, beat the yolks until pale and thickened, then scrape them onto the meringue and carefully fold together using a spatula. In two additions, sift the flour onto the meringue and gently fold together, trying to keep the mixture as light as possible. Transfer to a piping bag fitted with a 1.5cm (⅝in) plain piping tip. Draw a 20cm (8in) circle on a sheet of baking parchment, turn it over and put it onto a baking tray. Pipe the biscuit batter onto the paper using the circle as your template. Bake for 20–25 minutes or until a light golden brown. Leave to cool on the baking tray before peeling off the paper.

To make the ganache, put the cream and coffee in a small pan and bring to the boil. Remove from the heat and leave to infuse for 5 minutes, then strain out the coffee grounds through a fine sieve. Melt the chocolate in a heatproof bowl over a pan of gently simmering water, making sure the base of the bowl doesn't touch the water. Pour the infused cream over the chocolate, stirring together. Pour about one-third of the ganache into the pastry shell, spreading it over the base.

Trim the biscuit disc so when it is in the tart there will be a 1cm (½in) gap between the biscuit and tart shell. Put the biscuit, baked-side down, into the tart, then brush it liberally with the coffee. Pour over the remaining ganache, covering the biscuit. Transfer to the refrigerator for 1 hour or until the ganache has set.

To finish the tart, beat the mascarpone until light and creamy, then add the cream and icing sugar and whisk together until it holds soft peaks. Transfer the mixture to a piping bag with a large plain round piping tip. Pipe the cream into rounds over the tart and finish with a little dusting of cocoa powder. This tart will keep for up to three days in the refrigerator.

Fig and Star Anise Tart

Frangipane is one of those basic recipes that pops up a lot and is a great recipe to have on hand as it's very flexible. It can be used as the base for so many different recipes, including the classic Pear Tart (page 23) and in Almond Croissants (page 44), but in this recipe I am using it for a tart flavoured with fig and star anise. It's a classic pairing presented in a simple but beautiful manner, and is the sort of tart that is perfect to serve to friends at a dinner party; although it's a great dish to impress it's not difficult to make.

SERVES 10

½ recipe Pâte Sucrée (see page 158)
  or Pâte Brisée (see page 160), chilled
flour, for dusting

FOR THE FRANGIPANE
100g (3½oz) unsalted butter,
  at room temperature
100g (3½oz) caster sugar
2 large eggs
1 teaspoon vanilla extract
100g (3½oz) ground almonds
1 teaspoon ground star anise

FOR THE FIG FILLING
125g (4½oz) dried figs,
  roughly chopped
2 teaspoons sugar
3 small fresh figs

To make the frangipane, put the butter and sugar in a large bowl and beat together until light and fluffy. Add the eggs one at a time, followed by the vanilla. Add the almonds and star anise, and fold together using a spatula until smooth and fully combined. Set aside.

To make the filling, put the dried figs, sugar and 125ml (4fl oz) water in a small pan and bring to the boil over a medium-high heat, then simmer for 15–20 minutes or until the figs have softened and have absorbed the water. Using a fork, mash the mixture to form a smooth paste. Set aside to cool before using.

Roll out the pastry on a lightly floured work surface until it is 2–3mm (¹⁄₁₆–⅛in) thick. Gently drape the pastry into a 35 × 11cm (14 × 4¼in) loose-based tart tin, pressing it into the corners. Trim off the excess and prick the base of the pastry with a fork, then put it in the refrigerator for 30 minutes or until the pastry is firm.

Preheat the oven to 180°C (160°C fan/350°F), Gas Mark 4. Line the pastry with a piece of baking parchment and fill with baking beans or rice. Bake for 15 minutes, then remove the beans and parchment and bake for a further 5–8 minutes until lightly browned. Leave the pastry to cool for 5 minutes before continuing.

Spread the filling across the base of the tart and top with the frangipane, spreading it in an even layer. Trim the stems of the fresh figs and cut each in half, then press the halves, cut-side up, slightly into the frangipane. Return the tart to the oven and bake for 20–25 minutes until the frangipane is golden. Leave to cool completely before serving.

This tart will keep for up to two days in an airtight container, any longer and the pastry will soften.

Salambos

These little choux buns are a more unusual way of using the basic choux pastry recipe. They sit between an éclair and profiterole in terms of size but are filled and finished as you would for a Croquembouche (page 142): with a simple vanilla crème pâtissière inside and dipped in caramel that sets hard when cooled, giving you a great contrast in texture and flavour.

MAKES 10

FOR THE CRÈME PÂTISSIÈRE
½ vanilla pod or 1 teaspoon vanilla
   bean paste
250ml (9fl oz) whole milk
1 large egg
2 large egg yolks
100g (3½oz) caster sugar
25g (1oz) cornflour

FOR THE CHOUX PASTRY
30g (1oz) unsalted butter
pinch of salt
½ teaspoon caster sugar
45g (1½oz) plain flour
1–2 large eggs

FOR THE CARAMEL TOPPING
200g (7oz) caster sugar

For the crème pâtissière, halve the vanilla pod and scrape out the seeds. Put the seeds or vanilla bean paste in a large pan and pour in the milk. Put the pan over a medium-high heat and bring to the boil.

Meanwhile, put the egg, yolks, sugar and cornflour in a large bowl and whisk until smooth. Pour the boiling milk over, whisking constantly to combine. Pour this mixture back into the pan, return to a medium heat, and whisk constantly until thickened. Pour this custard into a clean bowl, then press a piece of clingfilm onto the surface, cool, and put it in the refrigerator until needed.

Preheat the oven to 180°C (160°C fan/350°F), Gas Mark 4 and line a baking tray with baking parchment. For the choux pastry, put the butter, salt, sugar and 4 tablespoons of water in a medium pan over a medium-high heat. Once the butter has melted and the mixture is at a rolling boil, add the flour and immediately stir together with a wooden spoon to form a rough paste. With the pan still on the heat, beat vigorously for 2 minutes, then tip the dough into a bowl and beat for a few minutes until it stops steaming.

Add one egg and beat until fully absorbed. Check the texture of the dough by seeing how the dough falls from the spatula. If it falls easily, forming a V-shaped ribbon, the dough is ready, but if the dough sticks to the spatula or is too thick, add the second egg, little by little, until the dough reaches the correct texture.

Transfer the dough to a piping bag fitted with a 1.5cm (⅝in) plain round piping tip and pipe the dough onto the prepared tray into 6cm (2½in) strips, leaving 2cm (¾in) between each salambo. Bake for 25–30 minutes until golden brown. Turn off the oven and leave the pastry to cool completely in the oven.

To finish the salambos, transfer the crème pâtissière into a piping bag fitted with a small plain piping tip. Use a sharp knife to make a hole in the base of each bun and then pipe in the crème pâtissière. Line a baking tray with a silicone baking sheet.

To make the caramel, put the sugar and 125ml (4fl oz) water in a small pan over a medium heat and cook until the sugar has dissolved and the mixture turns golden brown. Remove from the heat and allow the caramel to cool slightly until it has thickened to a dipping consistency. Very carefully, dip the top of each pastry into the caramel. Put the pastries, caramel-side down, onto the baking tray to set completely.

The pastries are best served on the day they are made, because the caramel starts to become sticky if left overnight.

Flan Parisien

This recipe is a classic that is seen in almost every pâtisserie, sometimes going by the name flan pâtissier. It is a homely, comforting recipe that is wonderfully simple to put together. No blind baking, just a simple crème pâtissière baked in a pâte brisée case. It reminds me of the custard tart I grew up with at home in Yorkshire, and it is also not too dissimilar in flavour to a Portuguese custard tart – custards definitely seem to be a universal idea.

SERVES 12

FOR THE CUSTARD FILLING
1 vanilla pod or 2 teaspoons vanilla
  bean paste
750ml (1⅓ pints) whole milk
225ml (8fl oz) whipping cream
3 large eggs
6 egg yolks
300g (10½oz) caster sugar
90g (3¼oz) cornflour

FOR THE PASTRY
Pâte Brisée (see page 160), chilled
flour, for dusting

To make the custard filling, cut the vanilla pod, if using, in half and scrape out the seeds. Put the seeds or vanilla bean paste in a large pan and add the milk and cream. Put the pan over a medium-high heat and bring to the boil.

Meanwhile, put the eggs and yolks in a bowl and add the sugar and cornflour. Whisk until smooth. Pour over the boiling milk mixture, whisking constantly. Return this mixture to the pan and whisk constantly until thickened, cooking for a few minutes extra to remove the taste of the cornflour. Pour this custard into a clean bowl, press a piece of clingfilm onto the surface, cool to room temperature and then put it in the refrigerator until needed.

Preheat the oven to 180°C (160°C fan/350°F), Gas Mark 4 and put a 23cm (9in) cake ring or a springform cake tin onto a baking tray. Roll out the pastry on a lightly floured work surface until about 2–3mm (1⁄16–1⁄8in) thick. Roll the pastry onto the rolling pin and gently unroll it into the prepared cake ring. Gently tease the pastry into the corners of the ring, then trim off any excess (see page 164).

Pour in the chilled custard and bake for 1 hour or until the custard is browned but still has a little wobble. Leave the flan to cool at room temperature for 30 minutes before transferring it to the refrigerator to chill.

The flan is best served chilled or at room temperature. It will keep for up to three days in the refrigerator.

Paris-Brest

Oddly for a pastry, this recipe is named after the Paris to Brest bike race, and was created in 1891 by a pastry chef who wanted to design a pastry to celebrate the race that went by his shop, hence the circle shape designed to look like a bicycle wheel. The race may no longer be part of the professional racing circuit, but the pastry has endured, becoming one of the most well-known pastries in France.

MAKES 8

Pâte à Choux (see page 156)
1 egg, beaten
50g (1¾oz) flaked almonds
icing sugar, for dusting

FOR THE CRÈME MOUSSELINE

1 vanilla pod or 2 teaspoons vanilla
  bean paste
500ml (18fl oz) whole milk
2 large eggs
4 egg yolks
200g (7oz) caster sugar
75g (2½oz) cornflour
250g (9oz) unsalted butter, diced
75g (2½oz) praline paste (homemade,
  see page 184, or store-bought)

To make the crème mousseline, cut the vanilla pod, if using, in half and scrape out the seeds. Put the seeds or vanilla bean paste in a large pan and add the milk. Put over a medium-high heat and bring to the boil. Meanwhile, put the eggs and yolks in a bowl and add the sugar and cornflour, then whisk until smooth. Pour over the boiling milk, whisking constantly to combine. Return the mixture to the pan over the heat, and whisk constantly until thickened, cooking for a few minutes extra to remove the taste of the cornflour.

Pour this mixture into a clean bowl and add half the butter, stirring to combine. Press a piece of clingfilm onto the surface of the custard, cool then put it in the refrigerator for 2–3 hours until fully chilled.

Preheat the oven to 180°C (160°C fan/350°F), Gas Mark 4 and line two baking trays with baking parchment. Using an 8cm (3¼in) cookie cutter, draw four rings onto the back of each piece of parchment. Transfer the choux pastry to a piping bag fitted with a large star tip (known as a French star tip). Pipe the choux into rings on the prepared baking trays using the circles as your template.

Brush the choux pastry with the beaten egg and sprinkle with the flaked almonds. Bake for 35 minutes or until golden brown. Turn off the oven and leave to cool in the oven for 30 minutes before transferring to a wire rack to cool completely.

To finish the mousseline, beat the remaining butter until light and creamy. Remove the pastry cream from the refrigerator and, using a whisk, beat the pastry cream to loosen it. Add a quarter of the pastry cream at a time, beating until smooth and fully combined after each addition. Add the praline paste and mix until fully combined.

To assemble the pastries, use a serrated knife to slice horizontally through the centre of the choux rings. Transfer the mousseline to a piping bag fitted with a large star tip and pipe the cream onto the base of the pastries. Place the tops of the choux rings on top of the mousseline. Dust with a little icing sugar and serve.

The pastry rings will keep for two days stored in an airtight container. The filling can be made and kept in the refrigerator for up to a week in advance.

TIP
The buns can be prepared a couple
of days in advance and filled and
decorated when ready to serve.

Coconut and Strawberry Choux Buns

To elevate the humble choux bun, chefs have started adding an extra element called craquelin, a simple crumble dough which turns the choux pastry into something much more elegant. By putting a disc of this dough onto the choux before baking, it allows the choux to expand perfectly, giving a rounded shape with the bonus benefit of adding some texture.

MAKES 20

FOR THE COCONUT CRÈME PÂTISSIÈRE
500ml (18fl oz) coconut milk
2 large eggs
4 egg yolks
400g (14oz) caster sugar
40g (1½oz) cornflour
2 teaspoons vanilla extract
a few drops of coconut extract

FOR THE STRAWBERRY COMPOTE
400g (14oz) ripe strawberries, hulled and roughly chopped
4 tablespoons caster sugar
2 tablespoons lemon juice

FOR THE CRAQUELIN
75g (2½oz) plain flour
75g (2½oz) caster sugar
60g (2¼oz) unsalted butter

FOR THE CHOUX PASTRY
Pâte à Choux (see page 156)

FOR THE DECORATION
400g (14oz) ready-made pouring fondant (see Resources, page 188)
200g (7oz) sweetened desiccated coconut

To make the coconut crème pâtissière, put the milk in a large pan over a medium-high heat and bring to the boil. Meanwhile, put the eggs and yolks in a heatproof bowl and add the sugar and cornflour, then whisk until smooth. Pour the boiling milk over, whisking constantly to combine. Return this mixture to the pan over a medium heat and whisk constantly until thickened. Pour into a clean bowl and add the vanilla and coconut extracts, stirring to combine. Press a piece of clingfilm onto the surface, cool, then fully chill the refrigerator for 2 hours.

To make the strawberry compote, put the strawberries in a medium pan and add the sugar and lemon juice. Cook over a medium heat until the sugar has dissolved, then cook for 5–10 minutes or until the strawberries have started to break down and the liquid has reduced to a syrup. Transfer to a jar or small bowl and chill in the refrigerator until needed.

To make the craquelin, mix the flour and sugar together in a small bowl. Add the butter and rub together using your fingertips until the mixture resembles breadcrumbs. Press together to form a small ball of dough. Put this between two sheets of baking parchment and roll out until 2mm (1⁄16in) thick. Put the sheet of dough on a baking tray and freeze.

Put the pâte à choux in a piping bag fitted with a 1cm (½in) plain round piping tip. Line two baking trays with baking parchment and draw ten 4cm (1½in) circles onto the back of each sheet. Using these as templates, pipe the choux into 20 rounds. Remove the craquelin from the freezer and, using a 4cm (1½in) cookie cutter, stamp out 20 discs and put one on top of each round of choux. Bake for 25–30 minutes until the craquelin is golden. Turn off the oven and allow the buns to cool in the oven for 30 minutes.

Use a small sharp knife to pierce a hole in the base of each bun. To assemble the buns, remove the crème pâtissière and the compote from the refrigerator. Beat the crème pâtissière to loosen it and transfer it to a piping bag fitted with a small plain piping tip. Put the compote in a disposable piping bag, and snip off the end. Half-fill a bun with the crème pâtissière, then pipe in some of the compote and finish off with more crème pâtissière, repeating with all of the buns.

To decorate the buns, put the fondant and desiccated coconut in two small bowls next to each other. Dip the top of each bun into the fondant, letting any excess drip off, before dipping into the desiccated coconut to coat the fondant. These are best served the day they are made, or the pastry will soften.

Éclairs

A little ignored, the flavours of éclairs were traditionally just chocolate, pistachio and coffee, but little else. Now there are pâtissieries opening that specialize in an array of amazing flavours, colours and designs. Here are two different ideas for fillings, a fresh and fragrant passion fruit and a rich speculoos filling, each is enough to fill one batch of éclairs.

MAKES 12

FOR THE CHOUX PASTRY
Pâte à Choux (see page 156)
1 large egg, beaten

FOR THE SPECULOOS AND MILK CHOCOLATE ÉCLAIRS
½ recipe Crème Pâtissière (see page 178)
150g (5½oz) speculoos spread or caramelized biscuit spread
200g (7oz) milk chocolate
100g (3½oz) speculoos biscuits

FORT THE PASSION FRUIT AND MILK CHOCOLATE ÉCLAIRS
100g (3½oz) milk chocolate
125ml (4fl oz) whole milk
1 large egg
2 egg yolks
100g (3½oz) caster sugar
25g (1oz) cornflour
125ml (4fl oz) passion fruit purée (approx. 8 fruit)
500g (1lb 2oz) ready-made pouring fondant (see Resources, page 188)
a little yellow food colouring
chocolate pearls or sprinkles

TIP
Choux pastry cooks to the shape in which it is piped, so the better you pipe, the better the shape of the finished éclairs.

Preheat the oven to 180°C (160°C fan/350°F), Gas Mark 4 and line two baking trays with baking parchment. Draw six 14cm (5½in) lines on the back of each sheet of parchment to act as your piping template.

Put the pâte à choux into a piping bag fitted with a 1.5cm (⅝in) plain round piping tip. To pipe, hold the piping bag at a 45-degree angle and, with the piping tip touching the baking parchment, pipe 12 straight lines. Brush each éclair with beaten egg, then bake for 25–30 minutes until golden brown and crisp. Turn off the oven and leave the éclairs in the oven to cool for 30 minutes.

For the speculoos version, combine the crème pâtissière and the speculoos spread, beating until smooth. Cover with clingfilm and chill until needed. For passion fruit éclairs, melt the chocolate in a heatproof bowl over a pan of gently simmering water, making sure the base of the bowl doesn't touch the water. Remove the bowl from the pan and leave to cool. Put the milk in a large pan over a medium-high heat and bring to the boil. Meanwhile, put the egg in a bowl and add the yolks, sugar and cornflour, then whisk until smooth. Pour the boiling milk over, whisking constantly to combine. Pour this mixture back into the pan, return to the heat and whisk constantly until thickened. (This will be thicker than a normal crème pâtissière, as it has only half the liquid at this stage). Pour into a clean bowl and add the passion fruit purée, mixing until fully combined. Pour in the melted chocolate and stir to combine. Press a piece of clingfilm onto the surface and chill in the refrigerator until needed.

To assemble the éclairs, use a sharp knife to make two holes in the base of each éclair. Put your chosen filling into a piping bag fitted with a 1cm (½in) plain piping tip and pipe into the éclairs. For the speculoos éclairs, melt the chocolate in a heatproof bowl over a pan of gently simmering water, making sure the base of the bowl doesn't touch the water. Meanwhile, put the biscuits in a small bowl and, using the base of a rolling pin, crush them into fine crumbs, then tip onto a flat plate. To finish, dip the éclairs into the chocolate and then coat them in the biscuit crumbs. Set aside until the chocolate has set.

For the passion fruit éclairs, soften the fondant in a heatproof bowl set over a pan of gently simmering water, or according to the pack instructions, until it becomes a dipping consistency. Add a little yellow food colouring and mix in well. Dip the éclairs into the fondant and, before the fondant sets, sprinkle with chocolate pearls or sprinkles.

Éclairs are best on the day they are assembled, but can be stored in an airtight container for up to three days, although the pastry will soften.

Cassis Religieuse

The religieuse gets its name because it supposedly resembles a nun's habit; the name has stuck, giving perhaps the most oblique name for a pastry. They are a little more involved than making éclairs – I think they are a labour of love, although well worth the effort.

MAKES 10

FOR THE BLACKCURRANT PURÉE
300g (10½oz) blackcurrants (fresh or frozen)
75g (2½oz) caster sugar
3 tablespoons crème de cassis

FOR THE CRÈME PÂTISSIÈRE
1 vanilla pod or 2 teaspoons vanilla bean paste
560ml (1 pint) whole milk
3 large eggs
6 egg yolks
300g (10½oz) caster sugar
75g (2½oz) cornflour

FOR THE CRAQUELIN
60g (2¼oz) plain flour
60g (2¼oz) caster sugar
50g (1¾oz) unsalted butter, at room temperature, diced

FOR THE CHOUX PASTRY
Pâte à Choux (see page 156)

FOR THE DECORATION
500g (1lb 2oz) pouring fondant (ready-made or powdered mix, see Resources, page 188)
a little purple gel food colouring
125ml (4fl oz) whipping cream, whipped to stiff peaks (you can also use leftover buttercream)

For the blackcurrant purée, put the fruit, 2 tablespoons of water and the sugar in a medium saucepan over a medium heat. Stir occasionally until the fruit starts to break down and releases lots of juice. Pour the mixture into a food processor and purée. Pour the mixture through a fine sieve into a bowl, add the crème de cassis and chill in the refrigerator until needed.

To make the crème pâtissière, cut the vanilla pod, if using, in half and scrape out the seeds. Put the seeds or vanilla bean paste into a large pan and pour in the milk. Put over a medium-high heat and bring to the boil. Meanwhile, put the eggs and yolks in a heatproof bowl and add the sugar and cornflour, then whisk together until smooth. Pour the boiling milk over, whisking constantly to combine. Pour this custard back into the pan, return to a medium heat, and whisk constantly until thickened. Pour the custard into a clean bowl and leave to cool slightly before stirring in the fruit purée. Press a sheet of clingfilm onto the surface and chill in the refrigerator until needed.

To make the craquelin, mix the flour and sugar together in small bowl. Add the butter and rub together using your fingertips until the mixture resembles breadcrumbs. Press together to make a small ball of dough. Put the dough between two sheets of baking parchment and roll out until 2mm (¹⁄₁₆ in) thick. Put the dough onto a baking tray and freeze.

Preheat the oven to 180°C (160°C fan/350°F), Gas Mark 4. Put the pâte à choux into a piping bag fitted with a 1.5cm (⅝in) plain round piping tip. Line two baking trays with baking parchment and draw ten 5cm (2in) circles on the back of one sheet and ten 3cm (1¼in) circles on the other. Pipe the dough onto the trays using the circles as your template.

Remove the craquelin from the freezer and, using cookie cutters 5cm (2in) and 3cm (1¼in) in diameter, cut out ten discs of each size. Put the craquelin discs on top of the corresponding rounds of pastry and bake for 25–30 minutes until the choux has risen and the craquelin is golden. Turn off the oven and leave the buns to cool in the oven for 30 minutes.

To assemble, make a small hole in the base of each bun. Put the crème pâtissière into a piping bag fitted with a 1cm (½in) plain piping tip and use to fill each bun. Soften the fondant in a heatproof bowl set over a pan of gently simmering water, until it becomes a dipping consistency. Add a little food colouring to create a light purple icing. Remove from the heat and dip in each of the buns. Transfer to a wire rack, putting a smaller bun on top of each larger bun, then leave to set. Put the whipped cream into a piping bag fitted with a small star piping tip and pipe a series of short strips as shown in the photo creating a 'collar'. Best eaten on the day they are made but they will be good for three days, although the pastry will soften. Store in an airtight container.

Millefeuille

The word millefeuille means 'a thousand layers', which makes me think the cake was named by a pastry chef who had a way with words. Puff pastry doesn't have quite so many layers, but I suppose it sounds better than 'Sept cents vingt-neuf feuille' – it doesn't quite have the same ring to it, does it?

MAKES 8

FOR THE CARAMELIZED PUFF PASTRY

1kg (2lb 4oz) puff pastry (Rough Puff Pastry, see page 162, or store-bought), thawed if frozen
flour, for dusting
4 teaspoons icing sugar, plus extra for dusting

FOR THE CRÈME LÉGÈRE

½ recipe Crème Pâtissière (see page 178), chilled
125ml (4fl oz) whipping cream

Line two baking trays with baking parchment. Divide the puff pastry into two pieces and, working with one at a time, roll out on a lightly floured work surface into a large rectangle about 2mm (1⁄16in) thick. Cut out a rectangle about 25 × 35cm (10 × 14in) and put onto the prepared baking tray. Repeat with the second portion of puff pastry. Cover with clingfilm so that the pastry doesn't dry out, then chill in the refrigerator for 1 hour before baking.

Preheat the oven to 200°C (180°C fan/400°F), Gas Mark 6. Put another sheet of baking parchment on top of the pastry and cover with another similar-sized baking tray (so that they are close fitting). This will help to weigh down the pastry so that it stays nice and thin. Bake for 25 minutes, then remove from the oven and take off the baking trays and parchment covering the pastries.

Increase the oven temperature to 220°C (200°C fan/425°F), Gas Mark 7. Dust each piece of pastry with 2 teaspoons of icing sugar in an even, thin layer. Return to the oven, uncovered, and bake for 10 minutes or until the sugar dissolves and caramelizes. Leave to cool on the baking tray for 5 minutes before transferring to a wire rack to cool completely.

Using a large, serrated knife, trim away the outside edge of each pastry sheet, then carefully cut each pastry down the middle into two long pieces. Cut each strip into six equal rectangles.

To make the crème légère (a lightened pastry cream), remove the crème pâtissière from the refrigerator and beat with a spatula to loosen it. In a separate bowl, whisk the cream until it just holds soft peaks, then add to the crème pâtissière and fold together. Put the crème légère into a piping bag fitted with a 1.5cm (5⁄8in) plain piping tip.

To assemble, pipe a layer of the cream over eight pieces of puff pastry. Top each with another piece of puff pastry and repeat. Finish by putting a third piece of pastry on top and dust it with a little icing sugar.

These pastries are best served within a few hours of assembling, but the pastry can be made up to 8 hours in advance and the crème pâtissière for the filling can be made up to three days in advance.

Simple Apple Tart

This is a great recipe for when you need something foolproof: something super-easy to put together that still tastes as though it has required time and patience to make. I prefer to serve this tart fresh from the oven with a scoop of homemade vanilla ice cream on top, melting as you bring it to the table – the perfect autumnal dessert.

SERVES 8

250g (9oz) puff pastry (Rough Puff Pastry, see page 162, or store-bought), thawed if frozen

flour, for dusting

juice of 1 lemon

3 large Granny Smith apples

1 large egg yolk, beaten

10g (¼oz) unsalted butter, chopped into small pieces

1 tablespoon caster sugar

vanilla ice cream, to serve

Preheat the oven to 200°C (180°C fan/400°F), Gas Mark 6 and line a baking tray with baking parchment. Roll out the pastry on a lightly floured work surface until it is about 2mm (⅛in) thick. Cut out a 23cm (9in) disc of pastry and put it on the prepared baking tray, then chill it in the refrigerator while you prepare the topping.

Put the lemon juice in a bowl and set aside. Working with one apple at a time, peel, core and thinly slice into wedges; this is easiest done with a mandoline, but you can also use a thin, sharp knife. Toss the apple slices in the lemon juice to stop them browning.

Once all the apples have been sliced, remove the pastry from the refrigerator and arrange the apples over the pastry in concentric circles, leaving 1–2cm (½–¾in) of the outside edge clear. Brush this border with the beatenegg yolk.

Dot the butter over the apples, and sprinkle the sugar over the top. Bake for 25–30 minutes until the pastry is golden brown. Leave to cool slightly before serving warm with a scoop of ice cream.

This tart is also delicious cold, but is best eaten on the day it is baked.

Apple Turnovers

The chausson au pomme – known in English as an apple turnover – is a wonderful breakfast pastry. Because it uses puff pastry instead of croissant dough, it is easier and quicker to make than most Danish pastries, especially if you are using ready-made pastry. The recipe I have developed is a take on the classic version, but I have also seen chaussons au pommes with raisins added to the apple mixture and even made with other fruits – a chocolate and banana version was a great twist.

MAKES 6

FOR THE FILLING
3 Granny Smith apples, peeled, cored and diced
20g (¾oz) unsalted butter
40g (1½oz) caster sugar
½ teaspoon vanilla extract
¼ teaspoon ground cinnamon

FOR THE CRUST
500g (1lb 2oz) puff pastry (Rough Puff Pastry, see page 162, or store-bought), thawed if frozen
flour, for dusting

To make the filling, put the apples, butter, sugar, vanilla and cinnamon in a medium frying pan and cook over a medium heat until the sugar has dissolved, the butter has melted and the apples have just started to break down. You still want plenty of texture, so don't cook until you have a smooth purée. Pour the compote into a bowl and set aside until cool.

Preheat the oven to 190°C (170°C fan/375°F), Gas Mark 5 and line a baking tray with baking parchment.

To form the turnovers, roll out the puff pastry on a lightly floured work surface into a rectangle roughly 45 × 30cm (17¾ × 12in). Using a small bowl or plate, 14cm (5½in) in diameter, cut out six rounds of pastry. Spoon some of the filling onto one half of each round, leaving 2cm (¾in) around the edges clear.

Brush the edges of the pastry with a little water and fold the pastry over, pressing the edges together to seal. Brush the top of the turnovers with a little water and put on the prepared baking tray, then put them in the refrigerator for 15 minutes. Use a knife to draw a pattern on top of the turnovers (a leaf design is classic) and bake for 30–35 minutes until golden brown. Leave to cool to room temperature before serving.

These pastries are best served on the day they are baked.

Kouign Amann

This pastry from Brittany is a thing of beauty. It uses a croissant pastry with added sugar so that as it bakes it caramelizes, similar to a palmier but even better and unbelievably delicious. Thanks to my quick croissant dough, it is now also very easy to make. Traditionally, it is made as one large cake, but in recent years it has become very common to see individual versions, sometimes referred to kouignettes, and this is the form I prefer. It is also one of the pastries that has jumped across the Atlantic to the US, where bakeries in New York and San Francisco are putting their own spin on the classic.

MAKES 10

4 tablespoons whole milk, lukewarm
125g (4½oz) plain flour, plus extra
  for dusting
125g (4½oz) strong white bread flour
7g (⅛oz) fast-action dried yeast
150g (5½oz) caster sugar, plus extra
  for dusting
½ teaspoon salt
225g (8oz) unsalted butter, chilled

TIP

If you don't have tart rings, you can also bake the dough in muffin tins. Simply grease them well with softened butter and press the formed pastries into the moulds. Bake as for the tart rings and, once baked, leave to cool in the tins for 5 minutes before removing them and leaving them to cool completely.

Put the milk and 4 tablespoons of lukewarm water in a medium bowl and mix to combine, then set aside. Put the flours, yeast, 30g (1oz) of the sugar and the salt into the bowl of a food processor and pulse to combine. Dice 125g (4½oz) of the butter into small pieces, about 1cm (½in) in size. Add to the food processor and pulse once or twice just to mix together. This is the most important stage: if the butter is mixed too much into the flour, the dough won't expand and puff up as it bakes, so it is better to err on the side of caution with the mixing. If you can't see chunks of butter, you have processed the dough too much. (Alternatively, mix all the dry ingredients together in a medium bowl. Add the diced 125g/4½oz butter, as above, and very lightly rub it into the flour, or use a pastry cutter. Do this briefly, just to start to combine it – as explained above, you still need to see chunks of butter.)

Tip the butter and flour mixture into the liquids and, using a spatula, fold the dry ingredients into the liquid, trying to combine everything without making the butter pieces any smaller. Once you have formed a rough dough, tip this out onto the work surface and very lightly work it into a ball of dough. Form the dough into a flat rectangle, wrap in clingfilm and put it in the refrigerator for 45 minutes.

Meanwhile, put the remaining chunk of butter in the freezer to chill it thoroughly (it needs to be hard).

Lightly flour a work surface and roll the dough out with the short edge facing you into a long rectangle three times as long as it is wide, about 15 × 45cm (6 × 17¾in) (although the exact measurements are not crucial). Brush off any excess flour. Take the butter out of the freezer and coarsely grate it over the bottom two-thirds of the dough.

Fold the top third of the dough over the middle third, then fold the bottom third over the other two-thirds, as if folding a business letter. This is known as the first turn. Wrap the dough in clingfilm and chill in the refrigerator for 20 minutes.

Remove the dough from the refrigerator and turn the dough 90 degrees so that the open ends are facing you. Repeat the rolling process and, before folding, sprinkle the dough with half the remaining sugar. Fold the dough into thirds as before and repeat this a second time. Wrap the finished dough in clingfilm and chill for 30 minutes before using.

Line two baking trays with baking parchment. Remove the dough from the refrigerator and cover the work surface with a small amount of caster sugar. Roll the dough into a 50 × 20cm (20 × 8in) rectangle. Using a sharp knife, trim the edges of the dough and cut the pastry into two strips and divide each strip into five equal squares.

Fold the corners of each square into the centre and press gently to secure in place. Put each pastry on the prepared baking trays, preferably inside 8cm (3¼in) tart rings (these help to give the pastries a better shape; if you don't have them, you can bake without them). Leave the pastries to rest for 30 minutes. Preheat the oven to 190°C (170°C fan/375°F), Gas Mark 5. Bake for 20–25 minutes until golden brown and the sugar has caramelized.

Remove from the oven and remove the tart rings, if using, then leave to cool on the tray. I serve these at room temperature when the sugar on the outside has set, giving you a wonderful texture.

Almond Croissants

A plain croissant is hard to beat, but the almond croissant comes oh so close to just surpassing it. Originally created as a way of using up stale, leftover croissants, almond croissants may be my favourite-ever recipe made from leftovers! I would happily let a batch of croissants go stale on purpose just so that I could make these. No one could call a croissant a healthy breakfast, and the almond croissant is no better, but as a treat every now and again they really are the best.

MAKES 8

8 stale croissants (homemade, see page 166, or store-bought)
75g (2½oz) flaked almonds
icing sugar, for dusting

FOR THE SOAKING SYRUP

100g (3½oz) caster sugar
2 tablespoons dark rum (optional)

FOR THE ALMOND FILLING

100g (3½oz) unsalted butter, at room temperature
100g (3½oz) caster sugar
2 large eggs
100g (3½oz) ground almonds
½ teaspoon almond extract (optional)

Preheat the oven to 180°C (160°C fan/350°F), Gas Mark 4 and line a baking tray with baking parchment. To make the syrup, put 200ml (7fl oz) water in a pan and add the sugar, then bring to the boil over a medium heat, and cook for 2 minutes or until slightly reduced. Add the rum, if using, and allow the syrup to cool completely.

For the filling, put the butter and sugar in a bowl and beat for 5 minutes or until light and fluffy. Add the eggs, one at a time, beating until fully combined before adding the next. Add the ground almonds and mix to combine. For a real flavour boost, add the almond extract.

To assemble, slice the stale croissants in half and dip each into the syrup, coating both sides of each piece. Transfer the filling to a disposable piping bag and snip off the end. Pipe a layer of the filling onto the bottom half of the croissant and sandwich together with the top half. Pipe a thin layer of the filling on top of the croissants and scatter over the flaked almonds. Bake for 15–20 minutes until the filling has set and just started to brown. Leave to cool completely, then dust with a little icing sugar before serving.

These pastries will keep for up to two days in an airtight container.

Pain au Raisin

I am in love with swirl pastries – for the taste, of course, but also because I find it adorable that some bakeries refer to them as escargots (snails), although I'm not sure I would want a real snail pastry for breakfast! This type of pastry is also wonderfully flexible. You can flavour it whichever way you choose: if you add some pistachio paste to the crème pâtissière and use chocolate instead of raisins, you have the pastry I almost always have when I step off the Eurostar in Paris, from my favourite boulangerie, Du Pain et des idées.

MAKES 8

75g (2½oz) raisins
Simple Croissant Dough
  (see page 166), chilled
flour, for dusting
¼ recipe Crème Pâtissière
  (see page 178)
1 large egg, beaten

Put the raisins in a small bowl and cover with boiling water, then set aside for 30 minutes. This will plump up the dried fruit and prevent them from burning as they bake. Drain and set aside.

Line two baking trays with baking parchment. Roll out the dough on a lightly floured surface into a rectangle about 24 × 48cm (9½ × 19in) with the short edge facing you, then trim the edges of the dough to square it off. Spread the crème pâtissière across the pastry leaving a clear border of 2.5cm (1in) along the far edge.

Sprinkle the raisins over the filling and then roll up the dough into a tight swirl, with the clean edge at the end of the roll. Cut into eight equal slices and put on the prepared baking trays. Lightly cover with clingfilm and leave to prove for 2–3 hours until almost doubled in size and puffy to the touch.

Preheat the oven to 180°C (160°C fan/350°F), Gas Mark 4. Brush the beaten egg over the top of the pastries, then bake for 20–25 minutes until golden brown. Remove from the oven and leave to cool on the trays for 5 minutes before transferring to a wire rack to allow them to cool completely.

These pastries are best eaten on the day they are made, but they can be refreshed the day after by reheating at 180°C (160°C fan/350°F), Gas Mark 4 for 10 minutes.

Apricot Danish

When a simple croissant won't hit the spot, a Danish pastry is the next step. It takes the same basic dough and gilds it with a little crème pâtissière. Finished with fresh apricot it makes the perfect weekend breakfast.

MAKES 8

Simple Croissant Dough
   (see page 166), chilled
flour, for dusting
¼ recipe Crème Pâtissière (page 178)
4 apricots, peeled, halved and stoned
   or 8 canned apricot halves (see Tip)
1 large egg, beaten
4 tablespoons clear apricot jam
80g (2¾oz) pistachio nuts,
   roughly chopped

Roll out the dough on a lightly floured surface into a rectangle roughly 24 × 48cm (9½ × 19in). Trim the edges and cut into eight squares, roughly 12cm (4½in) each. Fold the corners of each square into the centre and press down to secure them in place.

Line two baking trays with baking parchment and put the pastries onto the trays, then lightly cover them with clingfilm. Leave to prove for 2–3 hours until almost doubled in size – the dough should feel very delicate and spongy when lightly pressed.

Preheat the oven to 200°C (180°C fan/400°F), Gas Mark 6. Put the crème pâtissière in a piping bag fitted with a small plain round piping tip and pipe a round of the custard into the middle of each pastry, then cover each round of custard with a halved apricot, cut-side down. Brush the exposed dough with the beaten egg, and bake for 20–25 minutes until golden.

Remove from the oven and leave to cool on the trays for 5 minutes before transferring the pastries to a wire rack to cool completely. Once cooled, put the apricot jam in a small pan and bring to the boil over a medium heat. Brush the glaze all over the pastries and sprinkle the edge with the pistachio nuts.

The pastries are best served just warm or at room temperature on the day they are made. They can be refreshed the day after by reheating at 180°C (160°C fan/350°F), Gas Mark 4 for 10 minutes, although I doubt they will last beyond the first day!

TIP
To quickly peel stone fruit such as apricots, put them into a bowl of boiling water for up to 1 minute (ripe fruit will take less time). Remove and cool under cold water. Use the tip of a knife to loosen the skin, then peel it off.

Galette des Rois

A classic recipe served to celebrate Epiphany, galette des rois (kings' cake) is a simple pie consisting of an almond cream baked inside puff pastry. The tradition is that a small porcelain trinket is hidden inside the cream, and the person who finds it is named king for the day. As with most traditional recipes, it is also now served in many different flavours, but the basic form remains the same. For my version I have made individual cakes, but you could use this recipe to create one large cake cooking for 35–40 minutes or until golden brown.

MAKES 8

FOR THE RUM AND RAISIN FRANGIPANE
60g (2¼oz) raisins
4 tablespoons dark rum
100g (3½oz) unsalted butter,
  at room temperature, diced
100g (3½oz) caster sugar
2 large eggs, plus 1 large
  egg yolk for eggwash
100g (3½oz) ground almonds

FOR THE PASTRY
750g (1lb 10oz) puff pastry (Rough
  Puff Pastry, see page 162, or store-
  bought), thawed if frozen
flour, for dusting

Line two baking trays with baking parchment. To make the frangipane, put the raisins and the rum in a small pan over a medium heat and heat until the rum has been absorbed into the raisins. Tip into a small bowl and set aside to cool. Put the butter and caster sugar in a medium bowl and, using an electric mixer, beat until light and fluffy, about 5 minutes. Add the whole eggs one at a time, beating until fully combined before adding the next. Add the almonds and mix to combine. Mix in the rum-soaked raisins, then put it in the refrigerator until needed.

Divide the pastry into two pieces and roll out each on a lightly floured work surface until 2–3mm (¹⁄₁₆–⅛in) thick. Using an 8cm (3¼in) cookie cutter, cut out eight rounds of pastry. Using a 9cm (3½in) cookie cutter cut out another eight rounds of pastry.

To assemble, spread the frangipane onto the smaller rounds of pastry leaving 2cm (¾in) clear around the edge. Beat the egg yolk with 1 teaspoon of water and brush this eggwash around the edge of each pastry. Top each with a larger round of pastry, pressing the two pieces together to seal and place on the prepared trays. (Using a slightly larger piece of pastry for the top means that you can get a flush finish without stretching the pastry). Brush the pastries with the eggwash and put them in the refrigerator for 15 minutes. Preheat the oven to 200°C (180°C fan/400°F), Gas Mark 6.

Remove the trays from the refrigerator and, using a knife, draw a decorative pattern onto the tops of the pastries. Bake for 30–35 minutes until the pastry is golden brown. Leave to cool on the trays for 5 minutes before transferring to a wire rack to cool completely before serving.

These pastries are best served on the day they are made.

CHAPTER TWO

CAKES & DESSERTS

Gâteau au Chocolat

This cake has a simple decoration, but hiding underneath its coat of chocolate are multiple layers of chocolate sponge, sandwiched together with a rich dark chocolate mousse. It is a cake with plenty of elegance and the strength of flavour to back it up. You need to freeze it before glazing, so it's great if you need something that can be mostly prepared ahead of time.

SERVES 16

FOR THE CHOCOLATE SPONGE
butter, for greasing
60g (2¼oz) plain flour,
    plus extra for dusting
4 large eggs, separated
100g (3½oz) caster sugar
40g (1½oz) cocoa powder

FOR THE CHOCOLATE MOUSSE
400ml (14fl oz) whipping cream
200g (7oz) dark chocolate (60–70 per
    cent cocoa solids), finely chopped
100g (3½oz) caster sugar
3 large egg yolks

FOR THE GLAZE
300ml (½ pint) whipping cream
160g (5¾oz) dark chocolate (60–70 per
    cent cocoa solids), finely chopped
4 tablespoons golden syrup or
    clear honey

FOR THE DECORATION
100g (3½oz) dark chocolate (60–70 per
    cent cocoa solids), finely chopped

Preheat the oven to 180°C (160°C fan/350°F), Gas Mark 4 and grease and line three 20cm (8in) round cake tins with baking parchment. Grease the parchment and dust the inside of the tins with flour, tipping out any excess.

To make the sponge, put the egg yolks and half the sugar in a large bowl and, using an electric mixer, whisk for 5 minutes or until pale and thick. Put the egg whites in a clean, grease-free bowl and, using an electric mixer, whisk until they form soft peaks. Slowly add the remaining sugar while whisking until you have stiff, glossy peaks. Fold the whites into the yolk mixture in three additions. Sift over the cocoa powder and flour in three additions, folding lightly with a spatula until fully combined.

Divide the batter equally by weight between the prepared tins, gently spreading it to the edges. Bake for 10–12 minutes until the cakes are springy to the touch. Remove from the oven and turn the cakes out immediately, then leave them on a wire rack to cool completely.

To make the mousse, put the cream in a large bowl and whisk until it just starts to hold its shape and forms very soft peaks. Set aside until needed.

Melt the chocolate in a heatproof bowl over a pan of gently simmering water, making sure the base of the bowl doesn't touch the water, stirring occasionally. Remove from the heat, and leave the chocolate to cool slightly.

Put the sugar and 2 tablespoons of water in a small pan over a medium-high heat and bring to 120°C (248°F). When the syrup registers 110°C (230°F) on an instant-read thermometer, put the egg yolks in a bowl (this is best done using a freestanding electric mixer) and whisk on high speed until pale and thick. When the syrup has reached 120°C (248°F), remove from the heat and pour it onto the yolks with the whisk still running. Whisk for 2 minutes or until thickened and slightly cooled.

At this point the melted chocolate and the yolk mixture should both be at roughly the same temperature, which will make combining the two easier. Pour the chocolate into the yolk mixture and stir to combine. Add one third of the cream and fold together using a spatula, then repeat with the remaining cream.

To assemble the cake, trim the edges off the sponges to reduce their size a little. Line a baking tray with baking parchment and put a 20cm (8in) cake ring, or the ring from a springform cake tin, onto the tray. Put one sponge into the base of the ring and top with just under half the mousse, making sure it gets into the gap between the sponge and the ring.

Repeat with the second sponge and top with the last round of sponge. Top with the small remaining amount of mousse, spreading it out as smoothly as possible. Cover the top of the cake with clingfilm and transfer it to the freezer to chill overnight.

When you are ready to assemble the cake, remove the cake from the freezer and, using a kitchen blowtorch, or tea towel that has been soaked in hot water and wrung out, heat the ring around the cake to loosen it, allowing you to lift it off. Put the cake onto a wire rack set over a parchment-lined baking tray and set aside while you make the glaze. Don't leave the cake out for too long before glazing, because the colder the cake is, the better the finish will be.

To make the glaze, put the cream, chocolate and golden syrup in a large pan over a medium-low heat and cook, stirring regularly, until you have a smooth, shiny glaze.

Remove the glaze from the heat and immediately pour it over the cake, making sure the entire cake is covered. Leave the cake for 2 minutes so that the glaze can begin to set, then, using two sturdy palette knives, carefully lift the cake onto a cake stand or plate. Transfer the cake to the refrigerator and leave to defrost for a few hours before serving.

To make the decoration, melt the chocolate in a heatproof bowl over a pan of gently simmering water, making sure the base of the bowl doesn't touch the water, and stirring occasionally. Remove the bowl and pour the chocolate over the back of a baking tray, spreading it into a thin, even layer. Put the tray into the freezer for 2 minutes, or until the chocolate has almost set. Remove the tray from the freezer and, using a flat metal edge – something like a dough scraper or the long edge of a spatula – scrape the chocolate in a smooth motion away from yourself to create beautiful curls. (If you want to make the curls in advance, it is best that the chocolate is tempered, see page 186, but if you are putting them straight onto the cake, you can skip this.)

This cake will keep for up to a month frozen and unglazed; it will keep for up to a week once glazed, stored in the refrigerator. Simply remove from the refrigerator an hour before serving.

Lemon Pound Cake

Pound cake is one of the oldest and simplest cakes around, originally made with a pound each of butter, sugar, flour and eggs, and known in France as 'quatre-quarts'. This ratio can result in a cake that is a little too dense for most people's taste, so this version has been lightened and simply flavoured with lemon. My cake also uses soured cream, which gives it a wonderful moist and velvety texture. Although it's delicious on its own, I love to serve it lightly toasted with some crème fraîche and fresh berries.

SERVES 10

115g (4oz) unsalted butter, at room
  temperature, diced, plus extra
  for greasing
250g (9oz) caster sugar
zest of 2 lemons
1 teaspoon lemon extract (optional)
4 large eggs
225g (8oz) self-raising flour
125g (4½oz) soured cream

FOR THE LEMON GLAZE

3 tablespoons lemon juice (juice of
  1 lemon)
160g (5¾oz) icing sugar

Preheat the oven to 180°C (160°C fan/350°F), Gas Mark 4. Grease a 23 × 13cm (9 × 5in) loaf tin and line it with a strip of baking parchment. Put the butter, sugar, lemon zest and lemon extract (if using) in a large bowl and, using an electric mixer, beat for 5 minutes or until light and fluffy.

Put the eggs in a jug and whisk them together, then, working slowly, add the egg to the butter mixture, a little at a time, beating until fully combined before adding more. Once all the egg has been combined, sift in half the flour, mixing until just combined. Add the soured cream and mix until fully combined, then sift in the remaining flour and mix until just combined – don't over-mix, as it can make the cake tough.

Scrape the mixture into the prepared tin and gently level the top. Bake for 55 minutes–1 hour until golden brown and a skewer inserted into the centre of the cake comes out clean. Leave to cool in the tin for 10 minutes before inverting it onto a wire rack to cool until lukewarm.

To make the glaze, mix the lemon juice and icing sugar together in a bowl to make a thin, pourable glaze. Put a piece of baking parchment under the wire rack to catch the drips from the glaze. Pour the lemon glaze over the lukewarm cake, and use a pastry brush to spread it over the entire surface in an even layer. Leave the cake to cool completely on the wire rack before serving.

This cake will keep for 3–4 days stored in an airtight container; it can also be frozen for up to a month without the glaze.

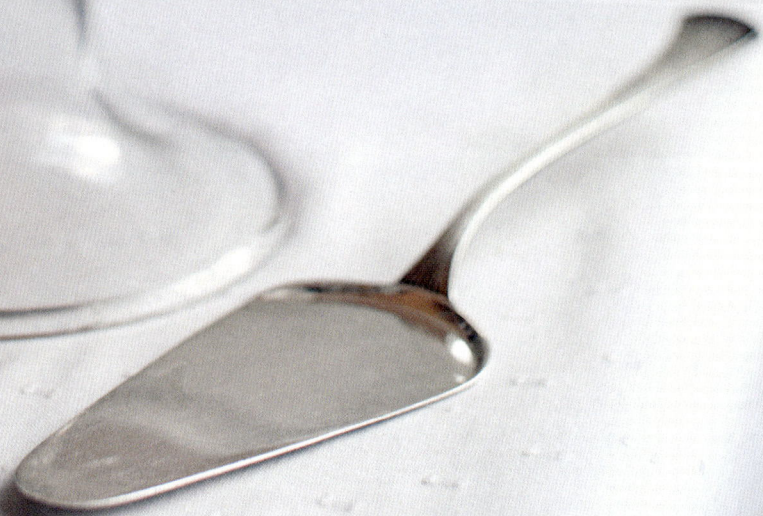

Fraisier

The fraisier is a simple and beautiful cake with a taste of summer, eaten when strawberries are at their best. Because this recipe really highlights the flavour of the fruit, it would be a disappointment to cut into this cake only to taste flavourless strawberries, so it really is worth waiting for the fruit when it comes into season, which makes the cake all the more special.

SERVES 12

FOR THE GENOISE SPONGE
20g (¾oz) unsalted butter,
  melted and slightly cooled, plus
  extra for greasing
3 large eggs
80g (2¾oz) caster sugar
60g (2¼oz) plain flour
15g (½oz) cornflour

FOR THE LEMON SYRUP
100g (3½oz) caster sugar
100ml (3½fl oz) lemon juice (from
  2–3 lemons)

FOR THE CRÈME MOUSSELINE
1 vanilla pod or 2 teaspoons vanilla
  bean paste
350ml (12fl oz) whole milk
2 large eggs
2 large egg yolks
150g (5½oz) caster sugar
50g (1¾oz) cornflour
2 teaspoons kirsch
200g (7oz) unsalted butter, diced

TO FINISH
300g (10½oz) strawberries, hulled
  and halved
100g (3½oz) white or green marzipan
icing sugar, for dusting

Preheat the oven to 180°C (160°C fan/350°F), Gas Mark 4. Lightly grease a deep 23cm (9in) round cake tin and line the base with baking parchment. To make the sponge, put the eggs and sugar in a large bowl and, using an electric whisk, beat on medium speed for about 8 minutes or until pale and thick, so that when the whisk is lifted from the bowl it forms a slowly dissolving ribbon that sits on the surface.

In a separate bowl, mix the flour and cornflour together and sift a third over the egg mixture, then very gently fold together using a spatula. Repeat this process with the other two-thirds of the flour mixture. Take a large spoonful of the egg mixture and add it to the butter, mixing them together until smooth. Tip this butter mixture into the bowl with the egg mixture and carefully fold it in to combine.

Pour the sponge mixture into the tin and gently level out the mixture. Bake for 20 minutes or until golden brown and coming away from the edges of the tin. Remove from the oven and leave to cool in the tin for 10 minutes, then invert the cake onto a wire rack to cool completely.

Meanwhile, to make the syrup, put the sugar and lemon juice in a small pan over a medium heat and bring to the boil to dissolve the sugar. Remove from the heat and set aside until ready to use.

Using a 20cm (8in) cake ring (or the ring from a springform tin) as a guide, trim the cooled cake so that it is 20cm (8in) wide. (I do this because I prefer to see the inside of the cake.)

To make the crème mousseline, cut the vanilla pod, if using, in half and scrape out the seeds. Put the seeds or vanilla bean paste in a large pan and add the milk. Bring to the boil over a medium-high heat. Meanwhile, put the eggs and yolks in a bowl and add the sugar and cornflour, then whisk until smooth. Pour the boiling milk over the eggs, whisking constantly to combine. Pour this mixture back into the pan, return to a medium heat, and whisk constantly until thickened, cooking for a few minutes extra to remove the taste of the cornflour.

Pour this mixture into a clean bowl and add the kirsch and half the butter, stirring to combine. Press a sheet of clingfilm onto the surface of the cream and leave it to cool, then put it in the refrigerator until chilled.

Put the remaining butter in a large bowl and beat until soft and creamy. Add a quarter of the custard at a time, beating it into the butter until smooth and fully combined. Transfer the finished mousseline to a disposable piping bag and snip off the end.

To assemble the cake, take the sponge and use a large, serrated knife to slice it into two even layers. Line a 20cm (8in) cake ring (or the ring from a springform cake tin) with a strip of acetate or baking parchment. Put the ring onto a serving plate or cake board and put the first layer of sponge inside, then brush it liberally with the lemon syrup. Put strawberry halves around the outside edge of the cake with their cut sides facing out. Pipe a layer of mousseline onto the cake layer, covering the sponge, then pipe into the gaps between the strawberries.

Roughly chop the remaining strawberries (reserving a few for decoration) and put on top of the mousseline layer. Top with the remaining mousseline and smooth it flat. Brush the second piece of cake with the remaining syrup and put it soaked-side down onto the mousseline-covered cake. Press it down to secure.

Transfer the cake to the refrigerator and chill for at least 1 hour before serving. When ready to serve, roll out the marzipan on a work surface lightly dusted with icing sugar to about 2–3mm (1⁄16–1⁄8in) thick, and cut out a disc to fit the top of the cake. Place the marzipan on the cake. To finish, decorate the cake with the reserved strawberries and dust with a little icing sugar.

A Genoise sponge cake is best eaten on the day it is made, but because this cake has been brushed with a simple syrup it will still be good the day after baking.

Milk Chocolate and Hazelnut Praline Bûche de Noël

The bûche de Noël is the classic French Christmas cake and, come December, pâtisseries go all out creating the most elaborate, beautiful versions you have ever seen. These high-end cakes can also be extremely expensive; I have seen them sell for as much as €120! My version might be simpler, but it is still an impressive Christmas cake, and much cheaper!

SERVES 10

FOR THE CHOCOLATE SPONGE
butter, for greasing
70g (2½oz) plain flour, plus
 extra for dusting
4 large eggs
100g (3½oz) caster sugar
30g (1oz) cocoa powder

FOR THE DECORATION
125g (4½oz) hazelnuts,
 roughly chopped
¼ teaspoon edible gold
 powder (optional)

FOR THE PRALINE BUTTERCREAM
50g (1¾oz) milk chocolate (30–40 per
 cent cocoa solids), finely chopped
125g (4½oz) caster sugar
1 large egg
2 large egg yolks
225g (8oz) unsalted butter, at
 room temperature, diced
4 tablespoons praline paste
 (homemade, see page 184,
 or store-bought)

FOR THE HAZELNUT SYRUP
40g (1½oz) caster sugar
2 tablespoons Frangelico

Preheat the oven to 180°C (160°C fan/350°F), Gas Mark 4 and grease a 33 × 23cm (13 × 9in) rimmed baking tray (known as a quarter sheet pan) and line with a sheet of baking parchment. Grease the parchment and then dust with a little flour, tipping out any excess.

To make the sponge, put the eggs and sugar in a large bowl and, using an electric whisk, beat until pale and thick, so that when the beaters are lifted from the bowl the batter leaves a trail. Put the flour and cocoa powder in a bowl and mix together. In three additions, sift this mixture over the egg mixture, gently folding together with a spatula until fully combined. Pour this batter into the prepared baking tray and gently level out. Bake for 10–12 minutes until the cake springs back to the touch.

Meanwhile, put a tea towel on a work surface and cover with a piece of baking parchment. Remove the cake from the oven and immediately turn it out onto the parchment. Peel off the parchment from the base of the cake, and then carefully roll the cake tightly, with the parchment and tea towel inside. Leave to cool, wrapped inside the tea towel, for 20 minutes. This will help the cake to unroll and re-roll later without cracking.

Put the hazelnuts for the decoration on a baking tray and toast them in the preheated oven for 10 minutes or until lightly browned. Set aside to cool.

To make the buttercream, melt the chocolate in a heatproof bowl over a pan of gently simmering water, making sure the base of the bowl doesn't touch the water. Leave to cool slightly.

Meanwhile, put the sugar and 75ml (2½fl oz) water in a small pan over a medium-high heat and bring to the boil. When the sugar has dissolved, cook until the syrup reaches 120°C (248°F) on an instant-read thermometer. When the syrup is around 115°C (239°F), put the egg and yolks in the bowl of an electric mixer fitted with the whisk attachment and whisk until pale and thickened (this is best done using a freestanding electric mixer). Once the syrup reaches 120°C (248°F), and with the mixer still running, carefully pour the syrup into the egg mixture. Continue whisking until the egg mixture has cooled to room temperature.

Add the butter, a few pieces at a time, beating until you have a silky smooth buttercream. Once all the butter has been added, add the praline paste and the melted milk chocolate, mixing to combine.

To make the syrup, put the sugar and 3 tablespoons of water in a small pan and bring to the boil over a medium heat, then cook for 2 minutes. Remove the pan from the heat and pour in the Frangelico.

To assemble, unroll the sponge and remove the baking parchment, then brush liberally with the syrup. Spread three-quarters of the buttercream evenly across the sponge, then carefully roll it up tightly. Carefully lift the roll onto a serving plate and spread the remaining buttercream in a thin layer over the outside of the cake. To make the decoration, put the chopped hazelnuts in a small bowl and mix with the gold powder, if using. Press the nuts onto the buttercream, coating the cake.

The cake is best eaten on the day it is made, but it will still taste great up to two days later as long as it is kept in an airtight container. The buttercream can be made up to a week in advance. Store it in an airtight container in the refrigerator. Allow it to come to room temperature and beat it until light and fluffy before use.

Almond Bostock

This is my absolute favourite way to use up leftover brioche. Once the bread has staled slightly, it is not the nicest to eat, but it makes a brilliant brunch dish. Bostock is brioche that has been soaked in a syrup flavoured with orange blossom and then baked with frangipane and flaked almonds. It's definitely worth sacrificing a few slices of freshly baked brioche for.

SERVES 8

8 slices brioche (homemade,
  see page 170, or store-bought),
  slightly stale
100g (3½oz) flaked almonds
icing sugar, for dusting

FOR THE FRANGIPANE
125g (4½oz) unsalted butter,
  at room temperature
125g (4½oz) caster sugar
1 large egg
125g (4½oz) ground almonds

FOR THE ORANGE BLOSSOM SYRUP
50g (1¾oz) caster sugar
1 teaspoon orange blossom water

Preheat the oven to 180°C (160°C fan/350°F), Gas Mark 4 and line a baking tray with baking parchment. To make the frangipane, put the butter and sugar in a bowl and, using an electric mixer, beat together for 5 minutes or until light and fluffy. Add the egg and beat to combine. Add the ground almonds and mix to combine. Set aside.

To make the syrup, put the sugar and 50ml (2fl oz) water in a small pan over a medium heat and bring to the boil, then reduce the heat and simmer for 2 minutes. Remove from the heat and add the orange blossom water.

To bake, put the brioche slices on the prepared baking tray, then brush the brioche liberally with the syrup. Divide the frangipane between the brioche slices and spread it into an even layer, right to the edges. Sprinkle the flaked almonds on top, then bake for 20–25 minutes until the frangipane is set and golden around the edges. Remove from the oven and leave to cool slightly. Dust with a little icing sugar and serve.

The bostock can be served up to three days after baking. Reheat in the oven at 120°C (100°C fan/250°F), Gas Mark ½ for about 10 minutes or until heated through before serving.

Banana Tarte Tatin

Tarte tatin is one of those recipes whose origin no one can quite agree on: was it a tart that was accidentally baked upside down, or was it created as a way of rescuing a pan of overcooked apples destined for an apple pie? What is known for certain is that it is named after the Tatin sisters who served the dish in the 1880s at their hotel in the centre of France, in Lamotte-Beuvron. It's normally made with apples that have first been caramelized and then baked with the pastry added on top, but my version is made with bananas, which need no pre-cooking, making this dish very quick to put together.

SERVES 8

250g (9oz) puff pastry (Rough Puff Pastry, see page 162, or store-bought), thawed if frozen
flour, for dusting
100g (3½oz) caster sugar
50g (1¾oz) unsalted butter
50ml (2fl oz) dark rum
3–4 ripe but firm large bananas

Preheat the oven to 200°C (180°C fan/400°F), Gas Mark 6. Line a baking tray with baking parchment. Roll out the puff pastry on a lightly floured work surface until it is about 2mm (⅟₁₆in) thick. Cut out a circle of pastry about 25cm (10in) in diameter and put it onto the prepared baking tray. Transfer to the refrigerator until needed.

If possible, use a 20cm (8in) ovenproof frying pan; otherwise the mixture can be cooked in a pan and transferred to a round 20cm (8in) cake tin. Put the sugar in the frying pan over a medium heat and leave, without stirring, until it has dissolved and lightly caramelized – it will caramelize further in the oven. (Be careful that it doesn't cook too far as it can burn easily.) Add the butter and rum, and cook until it is fully combined and smooth. If using a cake tin, pour this caramel mixture into the tin.

Slice the bananas into 2cm (¾in)-thick rounds and put them on top of the caramel in the frying pan or tin, leaving a small border around the outside. Put the pastry on top of the bananas, tucking the excess down the sides between the banana and the pan. Use a sharp knife to pierce the pastry a few times, and then bake for 35–40 minutes until the pastry is golden brown. Remove from the oven and leave to cool for 5 minutes before inverting the tart onto a plate to serve.

This tart is best served within a few hours of baking.

Gâteau Breton

The gâteau Breton is synonymous with the area it hails from, Brittany. It is a cross between a cake and a biscuit: dense, moist and utterly delicious. The version below, made with a prune purée, is the most popular, although I have also seen the cake made with many other fillings, including chocolate and caramel. It can also be served without the filling.

SERVES 12

FOR THE FILLING
100g (3½oz) pitted ready-to-eat
   prunes, roughly chopped
2 tablespoons rum

FOR THE CAKE
300g (10½oz) plain flour
200g (7oz) caster sugar
large pinch of flaked sea salt
250g (9oz) unsalted butter, at room
   temperature, diced, plus extra
   for greasing
6 large egg yolks

To make the filling, put the prunes in a small pan. Add 25ml (1fl oz) water and the rum, then heat over a medium-high heat until most of the liquid has been absorbed. Use a fork to mash them to make a thick purée, then cover and transfer to the refrigerator until needed.

To make the cake, put the flour, sugar and salt in the bowl of a food processor and pulse to combine. Add the butter and pulse until the mixture resembles breadcrumbs. (Alternatively, put the flour, sugar and salt in a large bowl and stir to combine. Add the butter and rub together using your fingertips, or use a pastry cutter, until the mixture resembles breadcrumbs.) Add five egg yolks and pulse, or stir with a fork, until the mixture forms a dough. Tip the dough onto a work surface and divide it into two equal pieces. Wrap the dough in clingfilm, and press each piece of dough into a flat disc. Transfer to the refrigerator for 2 hours or until firm.

Preheat the oven to 180°C (160°C fan/350°F), Gas Mark 4. Grease and line a 20cm (8in) round cake tin with baking parchment. Remove the dough and prunes from the refrigerator and put one portion of dough between two sheets of clingfilm or baking parchment. Roll out into a 20cm (8in) circle. Put this dough into the prepared tin, pressing it into the corners of the tin.

Spread the prune purée across the cake, leaving a 2cm (¾in) border around the outside edge. Roll out the remaining portion of dough, as before, into a 20cm (8in) circle and put it in the cake tin, pressing around the outside edge to stick the two pieces together and seal in the prune purée.

Whisk the remaining egg yolk together with 1 teaspoon of water and use this eggwash to brush over the top of the cake. Using a fork, score a crisscross pattern into the top of the cake. Bake for 50 minutes or until the cake is golden brown. (Cover with foil if the cake is browning too quickly.) Remove from the oven and leave to cool in the tin for 15 minutes, then invert it onto a wire rack to cool completely.

This cake will keep for up to a week stored in an airtight container.

Mixed Berry Charlotte

This cake always brings to my mind the court of the Regency era, with its elaborate style and fashions. The dessert was an invention of the chef considered the grandfather of French pastry, Marie-Antoine Carême, who named it after Princess Charlotte, the daughter of his former employer, King George IV.

SERVES 12

FOR THE BISCUITS À LA CUILLÈRE (SPONGE FINGERS)
3 large eggs, separated
100g (3½oz) caster sugar
75g (2½oz) plain flour

FOR THE RASPBERRY BAVAROIS
6 sheets gelatine
350g (12oz) raspberries
125ml (4fl oz) whole milk
6 large egg yolks
125g (4½oz) caster sugar
2 tablespoons crème de framboise
375ml (11fl oz) whipping cream

FOR THE DECORATION
400g (14oz) assorted berries

Preheat the oven to 180°C (160°C fan/350°F), Gas Mark 4. Draw a 20cm (8in) circle on a sheet of baking parchment, turn it over and put it onto a baking sheet. Draw two long rectangles 8cm (3¼in) wide on another sheet of baking parchment and turn it over on the tray.

To make the biscuits, put the egg whites in a clean, grease-free bowl and whisk until they form stiff peaks. Continue to whisk while you slowly pour in the sugar until the meringue is stiff and glossy. Beat the egg yolks in a separate bowl until pale and thickened, then scrape onto the meringue and fold together. In two additions, sift the flour over the meringue and gently fold together, keeping the mixture as light as possible.

Transfer the biscuit mixture to a piping bag fitted with a 1.5cm (⅝in) plain piping tip. Pipe a disc of mixture onto the baking parchment using the circle as your template. On the second tray, pipe strips inside the rectangles, making sure the strips are touching; you want two long strips to wrap around the mousse. Bake for 10–15 minutes until golden.

To make the bavarois, put the gelatine in a bowl and cover with ice-cold water. Set aside to soak. Put the raspberries in a food processor and pulse until smooth. Press the purée through a fine sieve to remove the seeds, and measure out 250ml (9fl oz) raspberry purée. Pour into a medium pan and add the milk, then bring it to the boil over a medium heat.

Put the egg yolks and sugar in a heatproof bowl and whisk until pale. Once the milk mixture has come to the boil, pour it over the yolks, whisking constantly. Pour this mixture back into the pan, return it to the heat and cook until it has thickened enough to coat the back of a spoon (or it reaches 75–80°C/167–176°F on an instant-read thermometer). Pour this custard into a clean bowl and add the crème de framboise. Squeeze the water out of the gelatine and stir the gelatine into the custard until dissolved. Cover the bowl with clingfilm and transfer it to the refrigerator until the mixture just begins to set.

Put the sponge disc onto a serving plate and put a 23cm (9in) cake ring (or the ring from a springform tin) over it. Take the strips of sponge fingers and trim off the base edges so that they will make a flush fit. Put the strips around the edge of the ring, cut-side at the base, trimming off any excess so that they sit snugly around the inside of the ring.

Pour the cream into a medium bowl and whisk until it just starts to hold soft peaks. Pour into the custard and fold together using a spatula. Pour into the ring and transfer to the refrigerator to set completely. To serve, carefully remove the ring and top with the berries. This cake will keep for up to two days in the refrigerator.

Amaretto and Peach Baba

The rum baba is a recipe with a wonderful history. It is thought to have been invented in the 18th century by Nicolas Stohrer, who was the pastry chef for the exiled king of Poland. Originally, the cakes were made with a sweet, fortified wine, and it wasn't until 100 years later that one of Stohrer's descendants added the rum. After the king's daughter married King Louis XV in 1725, Stohrer moved to Versailles. Five years later, he opened his bakery, which is now the oldest pâtisserie in Paris, and to this day it still serves the baba. To add my own spin on the recipe, I have used an Amaretto syrup and served the cakes with peaches.

MAKES 5–10

FOR THE BABA DOUGH

250g (9oz) plain flour
1 tablespoon caster sugar
1 teaspoon salt
7g (⅛oz) fast-action dried yeast
70ml (2½fl oz) whole milk
3 large eggs
70g (2½oz) unsalted butter, at room temperature, diced, plus extra for greasing

FOR THE AMARETTO SYRUP

200g (7oz) caster sugar
zest of 1 lemon and juice of ½ lemon
4 tablespoons Amaretto

TO SERVE

5 large peaches, peeled, stoned and diced
whipped cream

To make the baba dough, put the flour, sugar, salt and yeast in the bowl of an electric mixer fitted with the dough hook attachment and mix to combine. Put the milk in a small pan and bring to body temperature; test by dipping in your finger – it should feel the same temperature as the milk. Add the milk to the bowl followed by the eggs, and mix together on a medium-high speed for 5 minutes or until elastic. Add the butter, a couple of pieces at a time, mixing until thoroughly combined. Continue kneading until the dough is smooth and elastic – this can take up to 10 minutes, because of the butter and eggs.

Lightly grease ten dariole moulds with a little butter. Transfer the dough to a disposable piping bag, then snip off the end. Fill the prepared moulds half-full, then cover the whole batch with a sheet of greased clingfilm. Leave the dough in a warm place for 40 minutes–1 hour to prove until doubled in size.

Preheat the oven to 200°C (180°C fan/400°F), Gas Mark 6. Bake the buns for 10–15 minutes or until golden brown. Meanwhile, to make the syrup, put the sugar, lemon zest and juice and 250ml (9fl oz) water in a pan over a medium heat and bring to the boil, then simmer for about 5 minutes or until the mixture becomes syrupy and has reduced slightly. Remove from the heat and add the Amaretto.

Leave the buns to cool for 10 minutes, then remove them from the moulds and soak in the syrup for 10 minutes.

To serve, divide the diced peaches between ten serving glasses or bowls. Pour over some of the remaining syrup and top each with a bun. Serve with a little whipped cream.

TIP

If you want to make these ahead, they can be stored in a sealed sterilized jar with the syrup and will keep for up to a month. Made in dariole moulds this recipe will make five large babas but this dough can be used in classic baba moulds to make ten servings. You can also bake them in muffin tins, in fact any small mould will work.

Chocolate Fondants

Sometimes the old-fashioned recipes are the best – and you really can't get any more retro than this dessert. At one point a chocolate fondant was on the menu at almost every restaurant around. Although it's considered a bit of a cliché now, if you make these for friends at home, I guarantee that they will love them. You can't help but be impressed when you cut into the dessert and the molten centre oozes out.

SERVES 6

200g (7oz) unsalted butter, plus extra
    for greasing
1 tablespoon cocoa powder, plus extra
    for dusting
200g (7oz) dark chocolate (60–70 per
    cent cocoa solids), finely chopped
5 large eggs
125g (4½oz) caster sugar
100g (3½oz) plain flour
pinch of flaked sea salt
cream or vanilla ice cream, to serve

Preheat the oven to 190°C (170°C fan/375°F), Gas Mark 5 and line a baking tray with baking parchment. Grease six 7.5cm (3in) dariole moulds (or small ramekins) with butter and coat with a little cocoa powder, tapping out any excess. Put the dariole moulds onto the prepared tray and set aside.

Put the butter and chocolate in a heatproof bowl over a pan of gently simmering water, making sure the base of the bowl doesn't touch the water. Stir occasionally until fully melted. Remove from the heat and leave to cool slightly.

Put the eggs and sugar in a large bowl and, using an electric mixer, whisk for 8 minutes or until pale and thick. While still mixing, pour in the chocolate mixture, mixing until fully combined. Sift over the flour and cocoa powder, then add the salt and fold together using a spatula until you have a smooth batter. Using a ladle, divide the batter evenly among the prepared moulds, then bake for 8 minutes.

Remove from the oven and use a blunt knife to loosen around the edge of each mould. Immediately invert the fondants onto serving plates. Serve straight away with a little cream or vanilla ice cream.

The fondants can be prepared a day ahead and chilled until ready to bake. They can also be frozen and baked straight from the freezer – add 5 minutes to the cooking time.

TIP
If you want to put a modern twist on this classic dish, you can press 2 pieces of caramelized white chocolate into the fondant mixture just before baking (you will need about 100g/3½oz in total).

Pistachio and Cherry Soufflés

Soufflés have a reputation as being difficult desserts to prepare, but I think this is a little unfair. Yes, their success depends on gently folding in the egg whites, but with a careful hand this is not a difficult technique. Once you have mastered it, you can use your imagination to create all manner of flavours – another favourite of mine is a passion fruit soufflé with caramelized bananas.

SERVES 6

FOR THE CHERRY COMPOTE
300g (10½oz) dark cherries, pitted
   and halved
75g (2½oz) caster sugar
2 tablespoons lemon juice

FOR THE PISTACHIO SOUFFLÉ
room temperature butter, for greasing
125g (4½oz) caster sugar, plus extra
   for dusting
250ml (9fl oz) whole milk
4 large eggs, separated
30g (1oz) cornflour
50g (1¾oz) pistachio paste
   (homemade, see page 184,
   or store-bought)

To make the cherry compote, put the cherries, sugar and lemon juice in a medium pan over a medium-high heat and cook until the cherries have started to break down and the liquid has thickened and is syrupy. Pour the compote into a small bowl and put it in the refrigerator until needed.

To make the soufflés, take six 9cm (3½in) ramekins and brush the insides with butter. Add a little caster sugar, and turn the ramekins so that the insides are completely coated with it. Tip out any excess. Transfer the ramekins to the refrigerator and chill until needed.

Put the milk in a pan and bring to the boil over a medium heat. Meanwhile, put the egg yolks, 100g (3½oz) of the caster sugar, the cornflour and pistachio paste in a medium bowl and whisk together until smooth. When the milk is boiling, pour into the yolk mixture, whisking constantly. Pour this custard back into the pan and cook for 2–3 minutes, whisking constantly, until the custard has thickened. Pour the custard into a clean bowl, press a piece of clingfilm onto the surface, then put in the refrigerator until chilled.

Preheat the oven to 180°C (160°C fan/350°F), Gas Mark 4 and divide the cherry compote among the prepared ramekins. Put the egg whites in a large, clean, grease-free bowl and, using an electric mixer, whisk until they form soft peaks. Continue to whisk while you slowly pour in the remaining sugar until this meringue is stiff and glossy. Working in three additions, fold the meringue into the custard base using a spatula, folding until you can no longer see any streaks of white.

Using a ladle, divide the mixture between the prepared ramekins, filling to the top using a spatula. Scrape across the tops of the ramekins to remove any excess mixture and create a level top. Put the ramekins onto a baking tray and bake for 15 minutes or until well risen. Remove the tray from the oven, dust with a little icing sugar and serve immediately.

If you want to prepare these ahead, you can make the compote and the custard base up to three days in advance, then finish off the recipe when you want to serve the dish.

Clafoutis

This dish belongs to a category of French desserts based on a simple custard. Recipes such as the Far Breton (page 78) and even the Canelés (page 96) all use a variation on a thickened custard set with a little flour. The clafoutis is a classic dessert from the south-west of France and is traditionally made with sour cherries, but in the rest of France it is more commonly seen made with sweet cherries, at home you can use whichever variety you prefer.

SERVES 6

FOR THE BATTER

25g (1oz) unsalted butter, plus
   extra for greasing
250ml (9fl oz) whole milk
2 large eggs
75g (2½oz) caster sugar
50g (1¾oz) plain flour
zest of 1 large orange

FOR THE CHERRIES

300g (10½oz) sweet black cherries,
   pitted and halved
2 teaspoons caster sugar
1 tablespoon kirsch

Grease a 23cm (9in) round flan dish or cake tin. Put the butter and milk in a medium pan and bring to a simmer to melt the butter. Put the eggs, sugar, flour and orange zest in a medium bowl and whisk together until smooth. Slowly pour the milk over the egg mixture, whisking to combine. Press a sheet of clingfilm onto the surface of this custard and chill it in the refrigerator for at least 2 hours, or overnight, before baking.

Meanwhile, put the cherries in a small heatproof bowl with the sugar and kirsch, and stir to combine. Cover and set aside while the custard is chilling so that the cherries can macerate.

Preheat the oven to 180°C (160°C fan/350°F), Gas Mark 4. When ready to bake, pour the custard into the prepared dish or tin and scatter over the cherries. Bake for 30 minutes or until fully set around the outside and with just a slight wobble in the centre. Leave to cool before serving. I prefer to serve this lukewarm, but it is also great at room temperature or even chilled.

If you don't finish the dish, the leftovers can be kept in the refrigerator for up to two days.

Rice Pudding

A classic bistro dessert, perfect for the cold months of winter, rice pudding may well be the ultimate comfort food. I make my pudding on the hob rather than baking it in the oven, as I prefer the texture when cooked that way. To add a little extra luxury, I add two egg yolks towards the end of cooking to give it a richer taste, but these can be left out if you prefer.

SERVES 6

1 vanilla pod or 2 teaspoons vanilla
  bean paste
100g (3½oz) pudding rice or
  short-grain rice
1 litre (1¾ pints) whole milk, plus
  extra if needed
pinch of flaked sea salt
75g (2½oz) caster sugar or light
  brown sugar
2 large egg yolks (optional)
toasted flaked almonds, to decorate
  (optional)

FOR THE APPLE COMPOTE

25g (1oz) unsalted butter
50g (1¾oz) caster sugar
4 Granny Smith apples, peeled,
  cored and diced
1 teaspoon vanilla extract
¼ teaspoon ground cinnamon

Cut the vanilla pod, if using, in half and scrape out the seeds. Put the seeds and pod, or the vanilla bean paste, in a medium pan and add the rice, milk, salt and sugar. Bring to the boil over a medium-high heat, then reduce the heat and simmer gently for 35–40 minutes until the rice is tender and the liquid has reduced. Stir the mixture regularly to prevent a skin from forming.

Once the pudding is at your preferred texture, remove the pan from the heat and remove and discard the vanilla pod. Stir in the egg yolks, if using, then stir for a further 2 minutes to cook the egg. Pour into a bowl, press a piece of clingfilm onto the surface of the pudding and leave to cool, then put in the refrigerator until chilled. If, after chilling, you find the pudding is too thick, you can stir in a touch more milk to loosen it, if you like.

To make the compote, put the butter and sugar in a frying pan and cook over a medium heat until the sugar has dissolved. Add the apples, vanilla extract and cinnamon, and cook until the apple has started to break down, but stopping before you have a purée – you want some texture and bite left in the apple.

To serve, divide the warm compote between six glasses or bowls and top with the cold rice pudding, if you want to add some more texture, you could also finish with a sprinkle of toasted flaked almonds.

The rice pudding will keep for up to four days covered in the refrigerator.

Far Breton

A far Breton is a cooked custard that is thickened and set with flour, similar to the better-known Clafoutis (see page 76) but with a more robust texture. My favourite way to make this dessert is the way I remember enjoying it on holidays in Brittany when I was younger, with prunes that have been soaked in Armagnac, a flavour combination that is hard to beat.

SERVES 8–10

FOR THE CUSTARD
2 large eggs
2 large egg yolks
75g (2½oz)caster sugar
1 teaspoon vanilla extract
60g (2¼oz) unsalted butter, melted,
  plus extra for greasing
500ml (18fl oz) whole milk
100g (3½oz) plain flour

FOR THE PRUNES
200g (7oz) pitted ready-to eat
  prunes, halved if large
50ml (2fl oz) Armagnac
icing sugar, to serve

Put the eggs and yolks in a medium bowl and add the sugar, vanilla extract, butter and milk. Use a hand blender to process until smooth. Add the flour and blend again until smooth. Press a piece of clingfilm onto the surface of this custard mixture and put it in the refrigerator for at least 4 hours; this rest in the refrigerator helps to create the ideal texture. (You can also make the custard using a whisk, but make sure you only stir; try not to aerate the custard too much.)

Meanwhile, put the prunes in a small pan and pour over the Armagnac and 100ml (3½fl oz) water. Put the pan over a medium-high heat and cook until almost all the liquid has been absorbed. Remove from the heat and leave the prunes to cool completely.

Preheat the oven to 200°C (180°C fan/400°F), Gas Mark 6. Lightly grease a 25–30cm (10–12in) long roasting dish (or a deep 20cm/8in round cake tin) and line the base with baking parchment. Scatter the Armagnac-soaked prunes over the base of the roasting dish and then pour the chilled custard mixture over the top. Bake for 45 minutes–1 hour until puffed and browned around the edges and just set in the centre. Leave the custard to cool completely in the dish, then invert it onto a plate, peel off the baking parchment and turn the custard over onto another plate. Dust the custard with a little icing sugar to serve.

This dessert can be served lukewarm, but I prefer it at room temperature. Covered and chilled, it will keep for up to three days.

Crème Caramel

I find this dessert such a simple comfort. It might be the most basic of baked custards, but it really is heaven on a plate. Perhaps it is the memories of eating it as a child, or maybe it's the texture. Either way it is a delicious, classic dessert that deserves to be brought back from the annals of 'retro' and 'old-fashioned' to sit proudly on our dinner tables once again.

SERVES 4–6

FOR THE CARAMEL
100g (3½oz) caster sugar

FOR THE CUSTARD
1 vanilla pod or 2 teaspoons vanilla
  bean paste
400ml (14fl oz) whole milk
50ml (2fl oz) whipping cream
4 large eggs
125g (4½oz) caster sugar

Put four 9cm (3½in) ramekins or six 7.5cm (3in) dariole moulds in a roasting tin ready by the hob. Preheat the oven to 150°C (130°C fan/300°F), Gas Mark 2. To make the caramel, put the sugar and 3 tablespoons of water in a small pan over a medium-high heat, stirring occasionally, until the sugar has dissolved. Once the syrup is clear, stop stirring (as this can cause crystallization) and allow the sugar to caramelize. Once you have a caramel with a dark copper colour, remove the pan from the heat and immediately divide among the prepared moulds. (Be careful that the caramel doesn't cook too far as it can burn easily.) Set aside while you make the custard.

Cut the vanilla pod, if using, in half and scrape out the seeds. Put the seeds or vanilla bean paste in a medium pan and add the milk and cream. Heat gently over medium-low heat until the mixture is hot but not boiling.

Meanwhile, put the eggs and sugar in a heatproof bowl and whisk together until pale. Once the milk mixture has come to temperature, remove the pan from the heat and slowly pour the mixture over the eggs, stirring constantly. Using a ladle, divide this custard equally between the prepared moulds.

Put the roasting tin in the oven and add enough cold water so that it reaches halfway up the sides of the moulds. Bake for 20–30 minutes until the custards have set around the outside but still have a wobble in the centre.

Carefully remove the roasting tin from the oven. Lift out the custards and put them onto a wire rack to cool. Cover each mould with clingfilm then transfer them to the refrigerator to chill overnight. To serve, use a knife to gently loosen the custards from the moulds. Put a serving plate on top of each mould, and invert it to turn the custards out. Make sure all the caramel drains from the mould onto the custard.

The crème caramels will keep for up to three days stored in the refrigerator.

Crème Brûlée

It's childish I know, but one of the things I love about this dessert is the crack when you break through the caramel into the silky custard below – it's almost like breaking the seal on a new jar of coffee. It also provides a wonderful texture against that smooth, rich custard – a sophisticated dessert that is a breeze to put together.

SERVES 4

FOR THE CUSTARD

1 vanilla pod or 2 teaspoons vanilla
   bean paste
500ml (18fl oz) whipping cream
5 large egg yolks
45g (1½oz) caster sugar

FOR THE CARAMEL TOPPING

4 teaspoons caster sugar

Preheat the oven to 140°C (120°C fan/275°F), Gas Mark 1. To make the custard, cut the vanilla pod, if using, in half and scrape out the seeds. Put the seeds and pod or the vanilla bean paste in a medium pan and add the cream. Bring to the boil over a medium heat.

Meanwhile, put the egg yolks and sugar in a medium heatproof bowl and whisk for 5 minutes or until pale and thick. Remove the pan from the heat and take out and discard the vanilla pod. Slowly pour the cream into the yolk mixture, stirring constantly using a wooden spoon.

Divide the custard between four 9cm (3½in) ramekins and put into a roasting tin, spaced 2cm (¾in) apart. Fill the roasting tin with enough cold water to reach halfway up the sides of the ramekins. Bake for 30–40 minutes until the custards are just set; they should still wobble in the centre.

Carefully remove the roasting tin from the oven and take out the ramekins. Leave the custards to cool to room temperature, then transfer them to the refrigerator for at least 2 hours (or up to three days).

To make the topping, sprinkle 1 teaspoon of sugar in an even layer over each custard. Using a kitchen blowtorch, heat the sugar until it melts and caramelizes. (Alternatively, put the custards under a preheated hot grill and leave to caramelize, watching carefully that they don't burn.) Leave to cool. You can serve immediately or chill in the refrigerator to serve later as you wish.

TIP

This is a classic version of the dessert, but you can also flavour the custard in many other ways: you could infuse it with spices (adding along with the vanilla and pouring through a sieve when adding to the egg yolks), or add some chocolate, or even some praline paste (homemade, see page 184, or store-bought) simply by adding these to the finished custard and stirring until melted and combined. It is simply a baked custard, so by its nature it is very flexible.

Chocolate Mousse

When I was 18, some friends from university and I used our student loans to hop on the Eurostar and visit Paris for the first time. One evening we ate in a tiny little bistro somewhere in the 15th arrondissement. A small, cramped room it might have been, but it had the best atmosphere. For dessert we ordered chocolate mousse and, instead of an individual portion, we were presented with a huge bowl of mousse and were instructed to help ourselves – a great end to a brilliant meal.

SERVES 6–8

250g (9oz) dark chocolate (60–70 per cent cocoa solids), finely chopped
60g (2¼oz) unsalted butter
4 tablespoons strong black coffee
4 large eggs, separated
50g (1¾oz) caster sugar
2 tablespoons Amaretto, rum or brandy (optional)
whipped cream and crushed amaretti biscuits, to serve (optional)

Put the chocolate, butter and coffee in a heatproof bowl set over a pan of gently simmering water, making sure the base of the bowl doesn't touch the water. Leave the chocolate and butter to melt, stirring occasionally. Once you have a smooth mixture, remove the bowl from the heat. In a separate large bowl, whisk the egg yolks and the caster sugar together for 5 minutes or until the yolks are pale and thick. Add the alcohol, if using, and whisk to combine.

Put the egg whites in a clean, grease-free bowl and, using an electric mixer, whisk until they hold stiff peaks. Add the chocolate mixture to the egg yolks and mix to combine. Working in three additions, carefully fold in the egg whites using a spatula, folding until you can no longer see any streaks of white. Pour the mousse into a large serving bowl or divide among 6–8 serving glasses. Chill in the refrigerator for at least 4 hours to set. Serve topped with a little whipped cream and some crushed amaretti biscuits if you wish.

This dessert will keep for up to four days stored in the refrigerator.

Mont Blanc

As with most countries and their cuisines, you can see the influence of France's neighbours in its recipes and culinary past. French baking has been influenced by many countries in mainland Europe, including Germany, Poland and Italy. This dessert can originally be traced back to Italy, although it is now popular in numerous European countries, and especially in France. It is a simple dish of puréed, sweetened chestnuts with whipped cream, and it is most often served on top of a meringue. In my version I use a disc of sablé Breton instead, as I love the texture and flavour it lends to the dish.

SERVES 6

FOR THE SABLÉ BRETON
100g (3½oz) plain flour
pinch of flaked sea salt
¾ teaspoon baking powder
60g (2¼oz) caster sugar
2 large egg yolks
75g (2½oz) unsalted butter,
  very soft, diced

FOR THE CHESTNUT PASTE
120g (4¼oz) unsalted butter, at
  room temperature, diced
300g (10½oz) sweetened
  chestnut purée
4 tablespoons icing sugar

FOR THE CHESTNUT CREAM
225g (8oz) whipping cream
3 marron glacé, roughly chopped
icing sugar, for dusting, or edible
  gold leaf (see Resources, page 188),
  to decorate

For the sablé Breton, put the flour, salt and baking powder in a bowl and mix together, then set aside. Put the sugar and the egg yolks in a large bowl and, using an electric whisk, beat for 2 minutes or until the mixture is very pale and light. Beat in the butter, a little at a time, until the mixture is smooth and fully combined. Add the flour mixture and mix on a low speed until a dough just starts to form. Scrape the dough out onto a work surface and lightly knead until a smooth dough is formed. Put the dough between two sheets of baking parchment and roll it out until it is about 5mm (¼in) thick. Transfer the dough, still between its baking parchment, to a baking tray and chill in the refrigerator for at least 1 hour or until firm.

Preheat the oven to 180°C (160°C fan/350°F), Gas Mark 4 and line a baking tray with baking parchment. Remove the dough from the refrigerator and peel off the top sheet of baking parchment. Cut out rounds 8cm (3¼in) in diameter and put inside tart rings of the same size, set on the prepared baking tray. To get the six rounds of dough you will need to press the scraps of dough back together and roll out again. (If you don't have tart rings, you can bake the sablés without them on the prepared tray, but they will spread and will need to be cut back to size when baked.) Bake for 10–12 minutes or until golden brown. Leave the sablés to cool for 2 minutes then remove the tart rings and transfer the sablés to a wire rack to cool completely. (If you are baking the sablés without rings, as soon they come out of the oven use an 8cm/3¼in cookie cutter to cut them back to the correct size.)

To make the chestnut paste, put the butter in a bowl and beat until pale and creamy. Add the chestnut purée and icing sugar, and beat together until smooth. Transfer the paste to a piping bag fitted with a large multi-opening piping tip (often called a grass piping tip). If you don't have one of these, you can snip the very end off a disposable piping bag, creating a small hole.

Whip the cream until it holds firm peaks and then mix in the chopped marron glacé. Put a scoop of cream onto the centre of each sablé, and pipe the chestnut paste around the cream, then finish by dusting over a little icing sugar or topping with a little edible gold leaf.

The sablés can be made up to four days in advance and stored in an airtight container, but the remaining elements are best made close to the time of serving.

Île Flottantes

When I think of classic and elegant desserts, île flottantes is there, right at the top. It's beautiful in its simplicity. I considered changing this recipe to give it a modern twist, but in the end I decided that it's one of those dishes that needs no adornment and no changes. It has stood the test of time and is wonderful as it is.

SERVES 6

FOR THE CRÈME ANGLAISE

1 vanilla pod or 2 teaspoons vanilla
  bean paste
400ml (14fl oz) whole milk
100ml (3½fl oz) whipping cream
5 large egg yolks
80g (2¾oz) caster sugar

FOR THE POACHED MERINGUES

1 litre (1¾ pints) whole or
  semi-skimmed milk
3 large egg whites
100g (3½oz) caster sugar

FOR THE TOPPING

100g (3½oz) caster sugar
20g (¾oz) flaked almonds, toasted

To make the crème anglaise, cut the vanilla pod, if using, in half and scrape out the seeds. Put the seeds and pod, or the vanilla bean paste, in a large pan and add the milk and cream. Bring to the boil over a medium heat, then remove from the heat and set aside to infuse for 30 minutes.

Take out and discard the vanilla pod and bring the mixture back to the boil. Meanwhile, whisk the egg yolks and the sugar together until pale and thick. Continue to whisk the yolks constantly as you slowly pour the boiling milk over them. Pour this custard back into the pan over a medium heat and stir constantly using a wooden spoon until the custard has thickened enough to coat the back of the spoon (or until it reaches 75–80°C/167–176°F on an instant-read thermometer). Pour the custard through a fine sieve into a clean bowl, press a sheet of clingfilm onto the surface and put it in the refrigerator until needed.

To make the meringues, pour the milk into a wide, shallow pan and bring to a bare simmer over a medium heat. Meanwhile, put the egg whites in a clean, grease-free bowl and, using an electric mixer, whisk until they form soft peaks. Continue to whisk while you slowly pour in the sugar until this meringue is stiff and glossy. Put 12 large spoonfuls of meringue into the milk, a couple at a time, and poach for a few minutes on each side or until the meringue is firm. Using a slotted spoon, transfer the meringues to a plate covered with kitchen paper.

To serve, divide the chilled custard between six individual serving bowls and add the meringues. To make the topping, put the sugar in a small pan over a medium heat and cook, without stirring, until the sugar has dissolved and turned a dark golden brown. (Be careful that it doesn't cook too far as it can burn easily.) Carefully drizzle the caramel over the meringues and scatter the almonds over the custard.

The crème anglaise can be made in advance and stored in the refrigerator for up to three days.

Caramelized Pineapple Crêpes

Crêpes Suzette might be the classic crêpe dessert but these fine pancakes are also served with many other toppings and fillings, from sweet to savoury. They can make a great street food snack as well a wonderful end to a meal. My dessert takes the idea of a crêpe Suzette but uses caramelized pineapple to give a tropical twist.

SERVES 4

FOR THE CARAMELIZED PINEAPPLE
1 large pineapple
200ml (7fl oz) orange juice
100g (3½oz) caster sugar
1 star anise
20g (¾oz) unsalted butter
vanilla ice cream, to serve (optional)

FOR THE BATTER
150g (5½oz) plain flour
2 tablespoons caster sugar
¼ teaspoon salt
2 large eggs
300ml (½ pint) whole milk
30g (1oz) unsalted butter, melted
sunflower oil, for greasing

TIP
You can make the batter up to 1 day ahead, or the crêpes can be kept wrapped in clingfilm in the refrigerator for three days.

To make the caramelized pineapple, cut the top and bottom off the pineapple and cut away the skin, making sure to remove the 'eyes'. Cut the pineapple in half and cut out the core, then cut into slices, to make crescent-shaped pieces.

Put the orange juice, caster sugar and star anise in a medium pan, and bring to the boil over a medium heat. Remove from the heat and pour into a shallow container, add the pineapple, then put it in the refrigerator to marinate for at least 2 hours or up to 8 hours.

Heat a large frying pan over a medium heat and add the butter. When the pan is hot and the butter is bubbling, add the pineapple pieces in one layer (you will most likely have to do this in at least two batches, depending on the size of your pan). Cook on each side until the pineapple just starts to brown. Once all the pineapple has been caramelized, put it on a plate and set it aside. Pour the orange marinade into the pan and cook over a medium heat until it has reduced and is syrupy. Return all the fruit to the pan and remove from the heat, then set it aside until ready to use.

To make the batter, put the flour, sugar and salt in a medium bowl and whisk together to combine. In a jug, lightly whisk the eggs, milk and butter together, then pour it into the flour mixture, whisking until you have a smooth batter. Cover the bowl and put it in the refrigerator for at least 30 minutes before cooking.

When ready to serve, heat a 25cm (10in) frying pan over a medium heat until hot. Wipe with a piece of oiled kitchen paper. Pour in one ladleful of batter and turn the pan so that the entire base is covered in a thin layer. If the pan is hot enough, the crêpe should be cooked underneath within 30–40 seconds. Once the underside is a beautiful golden colour, carefully flip it over and cook for another 10-15 seconds until golden on the second side. Slide the crêpe onto a plate and keep it warm while you repeat until all of the batter has been used. (Don't worry if your first crêpe isn't perfect – this almost always happens to me, and it just becomes the chef's treat to test if I've made the batter correctly, of course!)

To serve, fold the crêpes into quarters and serve two per person with the warm caramelized pineapple and a scoop of vanilla ice cream, if you like.

Waffles

Although waffles might be more associated with France's neighbours in Belgium, they are actually a popular snack all across Europe. I like to think of waffles as the crêpe's big brother: a little more substantial with a crisp outside, but still light and fluffy on the inside. And, as with crêpes, they can be served with just about any topping, but here I'm sticking to a classic, hot chocolate sauce.

MAKES 12

FOR THE BATTER

325g (11½oz) plain flour
2 teaspoons baking powder
pinch of salt
60g (2¼oz) caster sugar
2 large eggs, separated
450ml (16fl oz) whole milk
1 teaspoon vanilla extract
100g (3½oz) unsalted butter,
  melted and cooled

FOR THE HOT CHOCOLATE SAUCE

75g (2½oz) cocoa powder
75g (2½oz) caster sugar
50g (1¾oz) dark chocolate (60–70 per
  cent cocoa solids), finely chopped

To make the batter, put the flour, baking powder, salt and half the caster sugar in a large bowl and whisk together. In a large jug, whisk together the egg yolks, milk, vanilla and melted butter, then pour it into the flour mixture, whisking until you have a smooth batter.

Put the egg whites in a clean, grease-free bowl and, using an electric mixer, whisk until they hold soft peaks. Continue to whisk while you slowly pour in the remaining sugar until the meringue is stiff and glossy. Add the meringue to the batter and gently fold together. Cook the batter according to your waffle maker's instructions.

To make the chocolate sauce, put 200ml (7fl oz) water in a medium pan and add the cocoa powder and caster sugar. Whisk together until smooth. Put over a medium heat and bring to the boil, then reduce to a simmer and cook for 2 minutes or until the syrup has thickened. Remove the pan from the heat and leave to cool for a few minutes, then add the chocolate and stir together until melted and smooth. You can serve the sauce warm or cold, but it gets a lot thicker as it cools down. If you have any sauce left over it can be kept in the refrigerator for up to a month and then reheated at a later point.

TIP

This recipe makes quite a lot of waffles, so you could, of course, halve the quantities, but you can also freeze the cooked waffles. Leave them to cool completely, then wrap them in a double layer of clingfilm. When you want to serve them, leave them to thaw fully before reheating them in the oven at 120°C (100°C fan/250°F), gas mark ½ for about 10 minutes or until heated through.

Canelé
2€

CHAPTER THREE

SWEET TREATS

Lemon Madeleines

I could talk about Proust and his love and affection for these cakes, I could talk about how well these go with a cup of tea, but all that has been very well covered many times before. For me, these little cakes are brilliant, because the batter can be prepared a couple of days in advance and then baked in no time at all – the perfect prepare-ahead recipe. They are also really versatile. I have flavoured them in all sorts of ways, from mixing cacao nibs into the batter to using a blood-orange glaze, and even dipping them in tempered chocolate. To get that characteristic shape there are a few things you can do to help. Firstly, chill the batter for at least 3 hours and chill the tray for an hour before baking. Secondly, don't overfill the mould, as this will result in a plain, domed madeleine without that classic hump. And thirdly, baking at a relatively high temperature also helps.

MAKES 12

2 large eggs
100g (3½oz) caster sugar
100g (3½oz) plain flour, plus
  extra for dusting
1 teaspoon baking powder
100g (3½oz) unsalted butter, melted
  and slightly cooled, plus extra
  for greasing

FOR THE LEMON GLAZE
zest and juice of 1 lemon
160g (5¾oz) icing sugar, sifted

Put the eggs and the sugar in a large bowl and, using an electric mixer, whisk until thick and pale, about 6–8 minutes. Put the flour and baking powder in a separate bowl and whisk together to combine. Sift a third of the flour mixture over the egg mixture, carefully folding to combine using a spatula, then add the remaining mixture in two additions in the same way.

Take a large spoonful of the batter and add this to a small bowl along with the butter, mixing them together to lighten the butter. Pour the butter mixture into the batter and gently fold together to combine. Press a sheet of clingfilm onto the surface of the batter, then put it in the refrigerator to chill for at least 3 hours before baking. (The mixture can be chilled for up to two days at this stage.)

To make the lemon glaze, put the lemon zest, juice and icing sugar in a medium bowl and mix together using a wooden spoon until you have a smooth, pourable glaze. Press a piece of clingfilm onto the surface of the glaze until needed – this will help to prevent it from forming a crust.

An hour before baking, grease a 12-hole madeleine tray very well and dust with a little flour, tapping out the excess. Transfer the tray to the freezer to chill.

Preheat the oven to 220°C (200°C fan/425°F), Gas Mark 7. When you are ready to bake, spoon the batter into the madeleine moulds. You don't need to spread it out, as this will happen as the madeleines bake. Bake for 8–10 minutes until the edges have started to brown. Remove from the oven and immediately turn out onto a wire rack. Leave to cool for 10 minutes, before dipping into the glaze, coating fully. Allow the excess to drip back into the bowl before setting on the wire rack, set over a piece of baking parchment, to set.

These are best served as close to baking as possible – they are great the day they are baked.

Canelés

A classic of the Bordeaux region, these were originally created as a way of using up the egg yolks left over from the winemaking process, as the whites are used to clarify the wine. It has also been suggested that in the past the flour used in this recipe was scavenged by local cooks when it was spilt from ships as they unloaded their goods – a great story.

MAKES 8–10

FOR THE CANELÉ BATTER
450ml (16fl oz) whole milk
3 tablespoons dark rum
1 teaspoon vanilla extract
100g (3½oz) plain flour
pinch of flaked sea salt
50g (1¾oz) unsalted butter
5 large egg yolks
175g (6oz) caster sugar

FOR THE COATING
30g (1oz) beeswax (available from health food stores or honey producers)
30g (1oz) unsalted butter

TIP
To make an authentic canelé with the correct texture, you do really need to use special copper canelé moulds. Unfortunately, these moulds are rather expensive, especially outside france. For this recipe I use 5cm (2in) canelé moulds, if you choose to use silicone canelé moulds they tend to be a little smaller, so you will get a few more canelés. You can buy silicone moulds for significantly less money, but I have yet to make a perfect batch with these. Look out for a mould that isn't flimsy and has a well-defined shape; you want a thick silicone mould that will hold the shape of the cake as the batter bakes.

The key to the perfect canelé is first to avoid aerating the batter and then to chill it for at least 24 hours, preferably 48 hours, before baking.

Pour the milk into a pan and bring just to the boil over a medium heat, then remove from the heat and add the rum and vanilla.

Put the flour, salt and butter in the bowl of a food processor and pulse until the mixture resembles fine breadcrumbs. Add the egg yolks and sugar and pulse, or stir with a fork, until fully combined. Turn the processor on and pour in the hot milk in a slow stream, stopping the processor as soon as the mixture is smooth. Pour the mixture through a fine sieve into a medium bowl. Press a sheet of clingfilm onto the surface of the mixture and leave it to cool, then put it in the refrigerator for a minimum of 24 hours, but preferably 48 hours. The reason for such a long rest is that it helps to settle the batter, reducing any air you may have added to it, and it also improves the texture of the finished canelés.

To prepare your moulds, preheat the oven to 190°C (170°C fan/375°F), Gas Mark 5 and put your copper or silicone moulds (see Tips) in the oven for 5 minutes to heat through. Put a small pan over a medium heat, add the beeswax and heat until melted. Remove the pan from the heat and add the butter, stirring until melted. Remove the moulds from the oven and use a pastry brush to coat the inside of the moulds with a thin layer of the beeswax mixture. Put the moulds upside down on a wire rack set over a sheet of baking parchment, and allow any excess to drip out. Once cooled, transfer the moulds to the freezer for 30 minutes.

When the batter has chilled, remove the clingfilm and scoop off any foamy layers that may have formed on the surface. Remove the moulds from the freezer and put onto a baking tray. Pour the batter into the moulds, leaving about 1cm (½in) clear at the top. Bake for 1¼ hours–1 hour 20 minutes until the canelés are a dark mahogany-brown colour – you want them just this side of burnt, giving the outside an almost bitter, caramelized crust. If after 30–40 minutes you find the canelés are expanding out of the moulds, remove the tray from the oven and, using a pair of kitchen tongs, gently tease back into the moulds. This is important because if the canelés don't sink back into the moulds the tops won't colour and caramelize properly.

Once baked, remove the tray from the oven and use kitchen tongs to turn the moulds over onto a wire rack. Tap out the finished canelés, then leave to cool completely before serving. For the finest texture, these are best eaten on the day they are made. They will be delicious for 1–2 days afterwards, but the crust will soften. Store in an airtight container.

Financiers

One of the reasons I love French baking is that many recipes have a wonderful backstory – some are a little far-fetched and some are very simple, but they are still a great explanation of where a recipe comes from. The financier falls into the latter category. A baker based in the financial district of Paris wanted to offer his customers, who were mostly bankers, a little treat that they could eat on the go without getting messy and covered in crumbs (if you've ever eaten a croissant you'll know all about this!). The financier was born, and its classic shape is also meant to represent a gold bar – another nod to the customers the product was aimed at. This is a very easy recipe, and the batter will keep for up to three days in the refrigerator, so it's perfect if you want to get everything prepped ahead.

MAKES 12

120g (4¼oz) unsalted butter, diced,
  plus extra for greasing
100g (3½oz) ground almonds
25g (1oz) plain flour
120g (4¼oz) icing sugar
pinch of salt
4 large egg whites
1 teaspoon vanilla extract

FOR CHERRY AND ALMOND FINANCIERS

12 sweet cherries, pitted and
  quartered
40g (1½oz) almonds, chopped roughly

These cakes can be baked in any small cake moulds such as muffin tins or silicone mini loaf pans (the cooking time below is for 12 cakes baked in silicone mini loaf pans).

Put the butter in a small pan over a medium heat and cook until the butter has foamed and then turned golden brown. Pour the browned butter into a small heatproof bowl and set aside.

Put the ground almonds, flour, icing sugar and salt in a bowl and mix together using a wooden spoon. Add the egg whites and vanilla extract, and stir to form a thick paste. Pour in the slightly cooled butter and stir until you have a smooth batter. Press a sheet of clingfilm onto the surface of the batter, then put it in the refrigerator to chill for at least 2 hours before baking.

Preheat the oven to 200°C (180°C fan/400°F), Gas Mark 6 and lightly grease your chosen moulds. Spoon the batter into the prepared moulds, filling them half-full. Bake for 12–15 minutes until they have started to brown around the edges. Leave to cool in the moulds for a few minutes before turning out onto a wire rack to cool completely.

The financiers will keep for up to two days stored in an airtight container.

For cherry and almond financiers, follow the recipe above, but once you have poured the batter into your moulds top with the cherries and almonds, then bake as above.

Brioche Suisse

A great way of using a basic brioche dough is to create a brioche Suisse. It's a rather delicious treat, usually served as a breakfast item – but really, when is it a bad time for brioche, custard and chocolate? I have provided a basic version here, but you can, of course, play around and make your own version. The custard can be flavoured in many different ways: you could use fruit purées in place of the milk or you could add some praline paste (see page 184); you could also use fruit as the filling instead of chocolate – it really is flexible.

MAKES 10–12

FOR THE BRIOCHE

180g (6oz) plain flour
180g (6oz) strong white bread flour, plus extra for dusting
20g (¾oz) caster sugar
1 teaspoon fine salt
6 tablespoons whole milk, lukewarm
7g (⅛oz) fast-action dried yeast
3 large eggs, plus 1 egg yolk for eggwash
150g (5½oz) unsalted butter, at room temperature, diced, plus extra for greasing

FOR THE FILLING

½ recipe Crème Pâtissière (see page 178), chilled
175g (6oz) dark chocolate chips, or roughly chopped dark chocolate (60–70 per cent cocoa solids)

Put the flours, sugar and salt in the bowl of your mixer fitted with the dough hook attachment and mix together to combine. Put the milk and yeast in a jug and mix together until the yeast has dissolved. Pour this mixture into the mixer followed by the whole eggs. Turn the mixer on to medium-low speed and mix together until a rough dough is formed. Knead, using the mixer, for a further 10 minutes until the dough is smooth and elastic.

With the mixer still on, add the butter, a couple of pieces at a time, mixing until fully combined. Once all the butter has been incorporated, knead the dough at a medium-low speed for 10–15 minutes until the dough no longer sticks to the sides of the bowl.

Put the dough in a large, lightly greased bowl and cover with clingfilm. Transfer the bowl to the refrigerator and leave to rise slowly for 8–10 hours.

Next morning, line two baking trays with baking parchment. Tip the dough onto a lightly floured work surface and roll out into a rectangle roughly 45 × 30cm (17¾ × 12in). Beat the chilled crème pâtissière with a spatula to loosen it, then, using a spoon or offset spatula, spread it over one half of the dough, along the longer edge. Sprinkle the chocolate chips over the custard, then fold the uncovered half of the dough over the custard and chocolate chips. Using a long, sharp knife, cut into 10–12 strips, depending on how large you prefer them to be.

Put the brioche strips onto the prepared baking trays, setting them about 5cm (2in) apart. Cover with lightly greased clingfilm and leave to prove in a warm place for about 2 hours until risen and puffy. To test the dough has proved fully, press with a lightly floured finger. If the dough springs back slowly, it is ready for baking; if it springs back quickly, it needs a little more time to prove. Preheat the oven to 180°C (160°C fan/350°F), Gas Mark 4.

Lightly whisk the egg yolk with 1 teaspoon of water and brush over the top of the buns. Bake for 15–20 minutes until golden brown. Remove from the oven and leave to cool on the baking trays for 10 minutes, then transfer to a wire rack to cool completely.

These are best on the day they are made, but they can also be frozen once fully chilled and this way they will keep for up to a month.

Breakfast Brioche Buns

Waking up to freshly made brioche has to be the best way to start the weekend. The smell of bread drifting through the house – hopefully mingling with the aroma of freshly brewed coffee – perfect! It's even better when I'm still in bed and someone else is doing all the work. This is a great way to use a basic brioche dough and makes for a brilliant breakfast pastry.

MAKES 8

FOR THE BRIOCHE DOUGH

180g (6oz) plain flour
180g (6oz) strong white bread flour
20g (¾oz) caster sugar
1 teaspoon fine salt
6 tablespoons whole milk, lukewarm
7g (⅛oz) fast-action dried yeast
3 large eggs, plus 1 for eggwash
150g (5½oz) unsalted butter, at room
  temperature, diced, plus extra
  for greasing

FOR THE FILLING

pearl sugar (see Resources, page 188),
  for sprinkling
½ recipe Crème Pâtissière
  (see page 178)
200g (7oz) blueberries, preferably
  fresh, but thawed frozen berries will
  also work

Put the flours, sugar and salt in the bowl of an electric mixer fitted with the dough hook attachment and mix together to combine. Put the milk and yeast in a jug and mix together until the yeast has dissolved. Pour this mixture into the mixer followed by three of the eggs. Turn the mixer on to medium-low speed and mix together until a rough dough is formed. Knead, using the mixer, for a further 10 minutes or until the dough is smooth and elastic.

With the mixer still on, add the butter, a couple of pieces at a time, mixing until fully combined. Once all the butter has been incorporated, knead the dough at medium-low speed for 10–15 minutes until the dough no longer sticks to the sides of the bowl.

Put the dough in a large, lightly greased bowl and cover with clingfilm. Transfer the bowl to the refrigerator and leave to rise slowly for 8–10 hours.

Next morning, lightly grease eight individual 10cm (4in) tart tins. Remove the dough from the refrigerator and press gently to knock it back. Divide the dough into eight equal pieces and form into rounds. Roll or press the rounds so that they are about 11–12cm (4½in) in diameter. Put the rounds of dough into the prepared tins. Allow the excess to go up the sides of the tins, as if lining with pastry. This creates a depression in the middle, which will later be filled with crème pâtissière and blueberries. Cover the buns with a sheet of lightly oiled clingfilm and leave in a warm place to prove for about 2 hours until almost doubled in size.

Preheat the oven to 180°C (160°C fan/350°F), Gas Mark 4. To test the dough has proved fully, press it with a lightly floured finger. If the dough springs back slowly, it is ready for baking; if it springs back quickly, it needs a little more time to prove.

Lightly whisk the remaining egg with 1 teaspoon of water and brush the ridge of the dough, then sprinkle over a little pearl sugar. Fill the depression in the dough with a layer of crème pâtissière and top with the blueberries. Bake for 20–25 minutes until the bread is golden brown in colour. Remove from the oven and leave to cool in the tins for 10 minutes, then carefully turn out onto a wire rack to cool completely.

These buns are best on the day they are made, but they can also be frozen for up to a month.

Tarte Tropézienne

Created by Alexandre Micka, a baker of Polish descent, this brioche-based recipe was famously given its name by the actress Brigitte Bardot, who had become smitten with the dish while she was filming in Saint-Tropez in 1955. Since then the recipe has been served at the eponymous pâtisserie – La Tarte Tropézienne – and such is its popularity that versions of the recipe appear in bakeries all across France, although the original bakery still claims it is the only one with the secret recipe. Classically, this is made as a large cake for sharing, but it is also sold in individual versions, which is how I have recreated it here.

MAKES 8

FOR THE BRIOCHE

180g (6oz) plain flour
180g (6oz) strong white bread flour, plus extra for dusting
20g (¾oz) caster sugar
1 teaspoon salt
70ml (2½fl oz) whole milk, lukewarm
7g (⅛oz) fast-action dried yeast
3 large eggs, plus 1 for eggwash
125g (4½oz) unsalted butter, at room temperature, diced, plus extra for greasing
pearl sugar (see Resources, page 188), for sprinkling

FOR THE CRÈME LÉGÈRE

½ recipe Crème Pâtissière (see page 178)
125ml (4fl oz) whipping cream

Put the flours, sugar and salt in the bowl of your mixer fitted with the dough hook and mix together to combine. Put the milk and yeast in a jug and mix together until the yeast has dissolved. Pour this mixture into the mixer followed by three eggs. Turn the mixer on to medium-low speed and mix until a rough dough is formed. Knead for a further 10 minutes, using the mixer, until the dough is smooth and elastic.

With the mixer still on, add the butter, a couple of pieces at a time, mixing until fully combined. Once all the butter has been incorporated, knead the dough at medium-low speed for 10–15 minutes until the dough no longer sticks to the sides of the bowl. Put the dough in a large, lightly greased bowl and cover with clingfilm. Transfer to the refrigerator and leave to rise slowly for 8–10 hours.

Next morning, preheat the oven to 180°C (160°C fan/350°F), Gas Mark 4 and line two baking trays with baking parchment. Remove the dough from the refrigerator and tip it out onto a lightly floured work surface. Divide into eight equal pieces and form into rounds, flattening each into a disc. Put the rounds onto the baking trays and cover with lightly greased clingfilm. Put the trays in a warm place and leave to prove for about 2 hours until risen and puffy. To test the dough has proved fully, press with a lightly floured finger. If the dough springs back slowly, it is ready for baking; if it springs back quickly, it needs a little more time to prove.

Lightly whisk the remaining egg and brush the buns to coat. Sprinkle the buns with pearl sugar, and then bake for 15–20 minutes until risen and golden brown. Remove from the oven and leave to cool on the baking trays for 5 minutes, then transfer to a wire rack to cool completely.

To make the crème légère, beat the crème pâtissière with a spatula to loosen it, then set aside. Put the cream in a bowl and whisk it until it holds soft peaks. Add to the crème pâtissière and fold together until fully combined. Using a serrated knife, slice the tops off the buns. Pipe or spoon the crème légère onto the base of each bun, then put the tops back on and gently press them until the cream reaches the edges.

As with all brioche recipes, these are at their best the day they are made; however, when left unfilled, the buns can be frozen for up to a month.

Sablés Breton

These little biscuits are a classic of the Brittany region, famous for its beautiful butter but also for its salt, which is harvested by hand in the salt marshes of Guérande. You can think of these as the French version of shortbread, but really the texture is a little different because of the way they are made. The recipe includes eggs that have been whisked until pale, giving the biscuits a light texture that is delicious on its own but also great used as the base for desserts, including my version of the Mont Blanc (see page 84).

MAKES 24 SMALL OR 10 LARGE SABLÉS

200g (7oz) plain flour, plus extra for dusting
pinch of flaked sea salt
1½ teaspoons baking powder
125g (4½oz) caster sugar
4 large egg yolks
150g (5½oz) unsalted butter, very soft, diced

Put the flour, sea salt and baking powder in a bowl and mix together. Set aside. Put the sugar and three egg yolks in a large bowl and, using an electric whisk, beat for 2 minutes or until the mixture is very pale and light. Beat in the butter, a little at a time, until the mixture is smooth and fully combined. Add the flour mixture and mix on a low speed until a dough just starts to form.

Scrape the mixture onto a work surface dusted with flour and lightly knead to form a uniform dough. Put the dough between two sheets of baking parchment and roll it out until it is about 1cm (½in) thick. Transfer the dough, still between its baking parchment, to a baking tray and chill in the refrigerator for 1 hour or until firm.

Preheat the oven to 180°C (160°C fan/350°F), Gas Mark 4. If making small sablés, lightly grease two straight-sided 12-hole muffin tins. If making the larger sablés you will need to grease ten individual 8cm (3¼in) tart rings and put them on a parchment-lined baking tray. (If you don't have tart rings, you can bake the sablés without them on the prepared tray, but they will spread and will need to be cut back when baked.) Put the remaining egg yolk in a small bowl and add 1 teaspoon of cold water, then mix together to make an eggwash.

Remove the dough from the refrigerator and peel off the top sheet of baking parchment. To make the small sablés, brush the dough with the eggwash and then use a fork to draw a crisscross pattern over the dough. Use a 5cm (2in) cookie cutter (or a cutter the same size as your muffin cups) to cut out as many rounds as possible, then put them into the muffin cups. If making the larger sablés, these are normally used as the base of a dessert, so they don't need to be eggwashed. Cut out rounds 8cm (3¼in) in diameter and put inside the tart rings (set on the prepared tray).

Bake the small sablés for 8–10 minutes and the larger ones for 10–12 minutes until golden brown. (If you are baking the large sablés without rings, as soon they come out of the oven use an 8cm/3¼in cookie cutter to cut them back to the correct size.)

Leave the sablés to cool in the tins for 2 minutes before either turning out the small sablés onto a wire rack or removing the tart rings and allowing the sablés to cool completely.

These biscuits will keep for up to a week in an airtight container.

Vanilla Sablés

This is the type of recipe where the ingredients are so simple and so few that quality really counts. Use the best you can find for a crumbly shortbread-style biscuit that has that wonderful buttery taste, for the perfect little cookie to nibble on in the afternoon. As with the Chocolate Sablés recipe (see page 106) the key is to mix in the flour only until it is just starting to combine, this way you will get that signature crumbly sablé texture.

MAKES 40

1 vanilla pod or 2 teaspoons vanilla
   bean paste
200g (7oz) unsalted butter, at room
   temperature, diced
175g (6oz) caster sugar
½ teaspoon flaked sea salt
2 large egg yolks
400g (14oz) plain flour
demerara or turbinado sugar,
   to decorate

Cut the vanilla pod, if using, in half and scrape out the seeds. Put the seeds or vanilla bean paste in a large bowl or the bowl of an electric mixer. Add the butter and, using an electric mixer, beat until smooth and creamy. Add the sugar and salt, and beat until light and fluffy, for a few minutes more. Add the egg yolks and beat until fully combined. Sift in the flour in one go and mix on slow speed until the mixture resembles sand or gravel; don't over-mix – it should not form a uniform dough.

Tip the mixture onto a work surface and use your hands to gently bring together into a uniform dough. Divide the dough in half and roll into two logs, 4cm (1½in) thick. Wrap in clingfilm and transfer them to the refrigerator to chill for 3 hours or until firm. (If you are in a rush, you can freeze the dough for 30 minutes or until firm.)

Preheat the oven to 160°C (140°C fan/325°F), Gas Mark 3 and line two baking trays with baking parchment. Remove the dough from the refrigerator and roll it in a few tablespoons of the demerara sugar, coating the entire outside of the logs. Using a thin, sharp knife, cut the dough into 1.5cm (⅝in)-thick slices and put onto the prepared baking trays. Bake for 20–25 minutes until very lightly browned around the outside. Leave to cool on the trays for 10 minutes, then transfer to a wire rack to cool completely.

These biscuits will keep for up to a week in an airtight container.

Chocolate Sablés

The chocolate sablé is the little black dress of biscuits: reliable, grown-up and with just a little hint of naughtiness! They take no time at all to make, but the rewards are bountiful. I use ½ teaspoon of sea salt in these biscuits, which might seem like a lot to some people, but salt and chocolate were meant to be together – salt highlights the chocolate flavour and enhances the overall taste. Just don't use table salt; you need a good flaked sea salt, such as fleur de sel. To dress up these cookies even more, I have dipped them in tempered chocolate and sprinkled them with cacao nibs, but this is optional – they are still a wonderful treat without it.

MAKES 40

FOR THE SABLÉ DOUGH
275g (9¾oz) plain flour
40g (1½oz) cocoa powder
¾ teaspoon bicarbonate of soda
½ teaspoon flaked sea salt
200g (7oz) unsalted butter, at room temperature, diced
50g (1¾oz) caster sugar
200g (7oz) light brown sugar
½ teaspoon vanilla extract
175g (6oz) dark chocolate (60–70 per cent cocoa solids), finely chopped

FOR THE COATING
250g (9oz) dark chocolate (60–70 per cent cocoa solids), tempered (see page 186)
cacao nibs, to sprinkle (optional)

Sift the flour, cocoa powder and bicarbonate of soda into a medium bowl and add the sea salt, then stir together. Set aside.

Put the butter in large mixing bowl and, using an electric mixer, beat until smooth and light. Add the sugars and vanilla extract, and beat together for 2 minutes until smooth. Add the dry ingredients to the bowl and mix together until you have a mixture that looks sandy (which is what sablé means in English), add the chocolate and mix to combine. The final dough should look almost like soil; it should not have formed into one large ball of dough. This is the key to getting the correct texture; mixed for too long the biscuits will be tough.

Tip out the mixture onto a work surface and gently press together to form a uniform dough. Divide in half and roll into two logs, 4cm (1½in) thick. Wrap in clingfilm and put them in the refrigerator to chill for 3 hours or until firm. (At this point you can freeze the dough for baking at a later date, or do as I do and bake one half of the dough and freeze the second.)

Preheat the oven to 180°C (160°C fan/350°F), Gas Mark 4 and line three baking trays with baking parchment. Remove the dough from the refrigerator and, using a thin, sharp knife, cut into rounds about 1cm (½in) thick. Put the biscuits onto the prepared baking trays, leaving 2cm (¾in) between each one. Bake for 10–12 minutes until set around the outside but still soft in the centre. Leave the biscuits to cool on the trays for 10 minutes, then transfer to a wire rack to cool completely.

Line a baking tray with baking parchment. Once the biscuits are cool, dip each one halfway into the tempered chocolate, allowing the excess to drip off. Put onto the prepared tray and sprinkle with a few cacao nibs before allowing the chocolate to set fully at room temperature, if you like.

The biscuits will keep for up to a week stored in an airtight container.

TIP
Although I have given a suggestion for the cocoa percentages of the chocolate used in this recipe it is purely a guide; you can use whichever chocolate you prefer. The key is to use one that you love.

Kougelhopf

If you visit Alsace, the first thing you notice is the beautiful medieval architecture. It is like stepping back in time – simply beautiful. The other thing you'll notice, if you're anything like me, is that the windows of boulangeries and pâtisseries are filled with the iconic local recipe, the kougelhopf. Based on a brioche dough, the kougelhopf is a wonderful recipe that has hints of rum, orange and plenty of raisins or currants. Although it is good at any time, I think it makes a perfect breakfast dish, as it's not too sweet and not too rich – and when you've had enough mornings that start with a croissant, this makes a wonderful change.

SERVES 12

FOR THE DOUGH
130g (4½oz) raisins
50ml (2fl oz) dark rum
30g (1oz) plain flour
300g (10½oz) strong white bread flour
30g (1oz) caster sugar
2 teaspoons fine salt
140ml (4½fl oz) milk, lukewarm
14g (½oz) fast-action dried yeast
5 large eggs
175g (6oz) unsalted butter, at room
   temperature, diced, plus extra
   for greasing
zest of 1 large orange
2 teaspoons orange flower water
   (optional)
50g (1¾oz) flaked almonds

TO FINISH
50g (1¾oz) unsalted butter, melted
icing sugar, for dusting

TIPS
* If you want to increase the sweetness a little, once you have brushed the kougelhopf with butter you can coat it in a thin layer of caster sugar, which adds both sweetness and texture, as it gives the outside a crisp finish.

* This recipe is traditionally made in terracotta moulds, but these are hard to find outside France. You can, however, find a metal version very easily, and you can also use a bundt-style mould if you prefer.

Put the raisins in a small pan and pour over the rum and 50ml (2fl oz) water, then cook over a medium heat until most of the liquid has been absorbed. Set the raisins aside until needed.

To make the dough, put the flours, sugar and salt in the bowl of an electric mixer fitted with the dough hook attachment and mix together to combine. Put the milk and yeast in a jug and mix together until the yeast has dissolved. Pour this mixture into the mixer followed by the eggs. Turn the mixer on to a medium-low speed and mix together until a rough dough is formed. Knead, using the mixer, for a further 10 minutes or until the dough is smooth and elastic.

With the mixer still on, add the butter, a couple of pieces at a time, until fully combined. Once all the butter has been incorporated, knead the dough, again at a medium-low speed, for 10–15 minutes until the dough no longer sticks to the side of the bowl.

Add the raisins, orange zest and orange flower water, if using, and mix until incorporated into the dough. Put the dough in a large, lightly greased bowl and cover with clingfilm. Transfer the bowl to the refrigerator and leave to rise slowly for 8–10 hours.

Once the dough has rested, grease the kougelhopf mould and scatter the flaked almonds into the base of the mould. Remove the dough from the refrigerator and press gently to knock it back. Form into a round and, using a wooden spoon, make a hole in the middle, about 2.5cm (1in) wide. Put the dough into the prepared mould and cover with clingfilm, then leave in a warm place to prove until doubled in size; depending on the temperature of the dough and the room, this can take about 2 hours.

Preheat the oven to 180°C (160°C fan/350°F), Gas Mark 4. To test the dough has proved enough, press with a lightly floured finger. If the dough springs back slowly, it is ready for the oven; if it springs back quickly, it needs a little more time.

Bake for 35 minutes or until the top of the bread is golden. Leave to cool in the mould for 5 minutes, then carefully turn the kougelhopf out onto a wire rack. While still warm, brush with the melted butter, then leave to cool completely before serving. To finish, dust with a little icing sugar.

Macaron à L'ancienne

Like a lot of older recipes, the story of macarons and their origin is the subject of debate. The story I prefer is that the recipe arrived in France courtesy of the pastry chef working for Catherine de Medici, an Italian noblewoman who married into French royalty in 1533. This would explain why macaron à l'ancienne, the old-fashioned form of macarons, so closely resemble amaretti, the Italian almond biscuit. Although the modern Parisian macaron has overtaken the original in terms of popularity, the macaron à l'ancienne can still be found in many towns across France and is seen as a speciality of towns such as Nancy and Saint-Émilion, the latter being one of my favourite towns in the south-west of France.

MAKES 45

2 large egg whites
pinch of fine salt
130g (4½oz) caster sugar
130g (4½oz) ground almonds
¼ teaspoon almond extract
2 tablespoons icing sugar

Preheat the oven to 160°C (140°C fan/325°F), Gas Mark 3 and line two baking trays with baking parchment. Put the egg whites and salt in a clean grease-free mixing bowl and, using an electric mixer, whisk until they hold stiff peaks.

Put the sugar, almonds and the almond extract in a large bowl and stir together. Add the egg whites and fold together to form a thick batter using a wooden spoon or spatula.

Transfer the batter to a piping bag fitted with a 1cm (½in) plain round piping tip. Pipe rounds of dough about 2.5cm (1in) in diameter onto the prepared baking trays. Dip a pastry brush into water and brush the tops of the biscuits to moisten them. Put the icing sugar in a small sieve and dust over the tops of the biscuits. Bake for 15 minutes or until the macarons have lightly browned.

Slide the baking parchment onto wire racks and leave the macarons to cool completely before peeling off the paper. Traditionally eaten as they are, the macarons can also be stuck together as pairs using a little melted chocolate.

The macarons will keep for three days stored in an airtight container.

Palmiers

I like to imagine that the palmier was originally created as a way of using up leftover pastry. It is such a simple recipe that it is hard to imagine that its two ingredients can actually produce something so tasty! You can flavour them however you wish. Classically, it is simply sugar, but you could also add cinnamon, chopped nuts or dried fruits. I use vanilla sugar, which I make myself by simply storing a couple of leftover vanilla pods in a pot of caster sugar and shaking it every now and again. After two weeks the sugar will have taken on all the aromas of vanilla.

MAKES 25

flour, for dusting
500g (1lb 2oz) puff pastry (Rough Puff
  Pastry, see page 162, or store-
  bought), thawed if frozen
75g (2½oz) vanilla sugar

Preheat the oven to 190°C (170°C fan/375°F), Gas Mark 5 and line two baking trays with baking parchment. Lightly flour the work surface and roll out the pastry into a rectangle, roughly about 35 × 25cm (14 × 10in). Trim the dough so that you have straight edges.

Sprinkle the dough with about 50g (1¾oz) of the sugar and gently press into the dough using a rolling pin. Roll the long edges of the dough into a tight log, meeting in the middle, creating the classic palmier look. Using a thin, sharp knife, cut the dough into slices roughly 1cm (½in) thick.

Dip both sides of the slices into the remaining sugar and put onto the prepared baking trays. Bake for 25–30 minutes until golden and caramelized. Resist the temptation to eat them straight away and leave them on the baking trays to cool to room temperature before serving.

These pastries are best served the day they are made, but they will still be good the day after baking if stored in an airtight container.

Chouquettes

This pastry is the simplest of recipes, using choux pastry as its base, and is the classic goûter treat: that wonderful French idea of having something sweet in the afternoon to hold you over until dinner. A basic choux pastry is topped with pearl sugar or sometimes with chocolate chips. It's as simple as it gets, but these pastries are oh so moreish. You often find them sold in little bags on the bakery counter, and I can imagine eating these as a child on the walk home from school.

MAKES ABOUT 30

60g (2¼oz) unsalted butter, diced
  into small pieces
½ teaspoon fine salt
1 teaspoon caster sugar
85g (3oz) plain flour
2–3 large eggs, plus 1 for eggwash
pearl sugar, for sprinkling
  (see Resources, page 188)

Preheat the oven to 180°C (160°C fan/350°F), Gas Mark 4 and line two baking trays with baking parchment. Put the butter, salt, sugar and 120ml (4fl oz) water in a medium pan over a medium-high heat. Once the butter has melted and the mixture is at a rolling boil, add the flour and immediately stir together with a wooden spoon form a rough paste.

With the pan still on the heat, beat vigorously for 2 minutes, then tip the dough into a bowl and beat for a few minutes more until it stops steaming. This dries the dough out, which helps it to absorb more egg, which in turn helps the choux pastry to expand properly as it bakes.

Add the eggs, one at a time, beating until fully absorbed before adding the next. Depending on the flour used and how much water evaporated as you made the dough, the choux pastry will need varying amounts of egg, so the above is given as a guide. I usually add two eggs and then very slowly start adding the remaining egg, checking the texture of the dough after each addition. You are looking for a dough that has a shine, and when it is lifted from the bowl it should fall from the spatula in a ribbon that forms a V-shape. If the dough doesn't have enough egg, it won't expand properly and will be prone to cracking as it bakes; if there is too much egg, the dough won't hold its shape and will collapse as it bakes.

Put the finished dough into a piping bag fitted with a 1cm (½in) plain round piping tip, and pipe into rounds on the prepared baking trays, about 2.5cm (1in) in diameter. Lightly whisk the remaining egg to create an eggwash and use to lightly brush the rounds of dough. Sprinkle liberally with the pearl sugar and bake for 35 minutes or until golden brown. Turn off the oven and allow the chouquettes to cool in the oven for 20 minutes, then transfer them to a wire rack to cool completely.

As with all choux pastry recipes, these are really best on the day they are made, but they will still be very enjoyable the day after, although just a little softer. Store in an airtight container.

Pâte de Fruit

Pâte de fruit translates as 'fruit paste'. Hardly the most mouthwatering name, but the taste is intense and they look fantastically vivid, like little fruit jewels, and they are also surprisingly easy to make. To get the best jellies, use fruits that are in season so that they are full of flavour. This recipe makes quite a lot, so why not whip up a batch and give some to a friend? They will definitely appreciate it!

MAKES 60 PER BATCH

FOR THE RASPBERRY PÂTE DE FRUIT

600g (1lb 5oz) raspberries
butter or oil, preferably an oil spray,
   for greasing
1 tablespoon lemon juice
400g (14oz) caster sugar
2 tablespoons liquid pectin
125g (4½oz) granulated sugar,
   for coating

FOR THE MANGO PÂTE DE FRUIT

3 large mangoes
butter or oil, preferably an oil spray,
   for greasing
1 tablespoon lemon juice
400g (14oz) caster sugar
2½ tablespoons liquid pectin
125g (4½oz) granulated sugar,
   for coating

The process for both flavours is essentially the same. For the raspberry flavour, put the raspberries into a food processor and process until puréed. Pass through a fine sieve to remove the seeds, and measure out 400ml (14fl oz) of the liquid. For the mango, peel the mangoes and cut the fruit off the pit. Put the fruit into a food processor and process until smooth. Pour through a sieve to remove any stringy bits and measure out 400ml (14fl oz) of the purée.

Lightly grease a 20cm (8in) square tin and line with baking parchment, making sure the paper overhangs the tin. Lightly grease the parchment. Put this by the hob, so that it is close by and ready to use.

Put the fruit purée, lemon juice and sugar in a medium pan and cook over a medium-high heat until it reaches 107°C (225°F), stirring occasionally to stop the mixture from scorching. Once the mixture is at temperature, stir in the pectin and cook for a further minute, then remove from the heat and immediately pour into the prepared tin. Leave to set for 2 hours, then transfer to the refrigerator to chill overnight.

Once fully set, use the overhanging parchment to lift the pâte de fruit out of the tin and place on a chopping board. Using a thin, sharp knife, cut into squares and coat in the granulated sugar.

The pâte de fruit will keep for up to a week in an airtight container.

Orangettes

An elegant, sweet recipe, these chocolate-dipped candied orange strips make a wonderful Christmas gift. Just ensure that you make extra, as you will definitely want to keep some for yourself. Although I have made these with orange peel, as is traditional, they can be made with the peel of all different types of citrus fruit – grapefruit makes a wonderful alternative.

MAKES ABOUT 60

FOR THE CANDIED PEEL
4 large navel oranges
400g (14oz) caster sugar

FOR THE COATING
75g (2½oz) caster sugar
150g (5½oz) dark chocolate
 (60–70 per cent cocoa solids),
 tempered (see page 186)

To make the candied peel, slice off both ends of the oranges with a sharp knife, and then use the knife to score the peel into quarters. Carefully remove the peel from the fruit and then cut into strips. Put the peel in a medium pan and cover with cold water. Set the pan over a high heat and bring to the boil, then simmer for 2 minutes to blanch the peel. Drain off the boiling water. Repeat this process another three times. This helps to reduce the bitterness in the fruit.

Set the peel aside and put the sugar for the peel in the pan and add 400ml (14fl oz) water. Bring to the boil over a medium-high heat. Add the orange peel and reduce the heat to a simmer, then cook for up to 1 hour or until the peel is translucent. Using a pair of tongs, lift the peel from the syrup and put it onto a piece of baking parchment. (You can keep the leftover syrup and use it in cocktails.)

Leave the peel to dry for at least 4 hours or until the syrup has become tacky. Put the sugar for coating in a small bowl and toss in the peel to coat thoroughly. Put the sugar-coated peel onto a clean sheet of baking parchment and leave to dry out overnight.

If you want the peel to last and make a great gift, then it is best to temper the chocolate, as this means the orangettes won't need to be chilled and will keep for months, although I guarantee they won't last that long! Put the tempered chocolate into a small bowl or glass and dip in the peel, coating half of each piece with chocolate. Allow the excess to drip off and then put the coated peel onto a piece of baking parchment. Leave the chocolate to set at room temperature.

The orangettes will keep for up to two months, stored in an airtight container.

Caramels

These are little nuggets of addictive sweetness: the original salted caramel – the classic that started a modern trend. Salted butter caramels hail from Brittany, a region famous for its butter, my favourite of which is studded with flecks of sea salt. This mixture of butter and sea salt makes a caramel that is, for me, perfection. The key to a soft caramel is cooking to the correct temperature, and I find an accurate instant-read thermometer is a great help.

MAKES 30

100g (3½oz) unsalted butter, diced, plus extra for greasing
300g (10½oz) caster sugar
150ml (¼ pint) double cream
2 teaspoons flaked sea salt

SALTED BUTTER CARAMELS

Lightly grease a 23 × 13cm (9 × 5in) loaf tin (the exact size is not crucial) and line with foil or baking parchment, then grease the lining. Have this ready by the hob, so that it is right by you when the caramel reaches the correct temperature. Put the sugar in a medium, heavy-based pan over a medium heat and cook, without stirring, until the sugar is a dark copper-caramel colour.

Meanwhile, warm the cream in a small pan over a medium heat. When the sugar has cooked to the correct colour, remove the pan from the heat and carefully add half the cream – this will bubble up violently, so pour slowly. Once the bubbling has settled, pour in the remaining cream and add the butter and salt. Cook the caramel until it reaches 122°C (252°F), then immediately remove the pan from the heat and pour the mixture into the prepared tin. Leave to set for at least 4 hours.

Turn the set caramel onto a chopping board and peel off the paper, then, using a thin, sharp knife, cut into squares or your chosen shape. These caramels will keep for up to a week wrapped in baking parchment and stored in an airtight container.

MAKES 30

150ml (¼ pint) double cream, plus extra if needed
2 chai teabags
2 teaspoons ground cinnamon
1 teaspoon ground ginger
300g (10½oz) caster sugar
100g (3½oz) unsalted butter, diced

CHAI TEA CARAMELS

Pour the cream into a small pan and add the teabags, cinnamon and ginger, then bring to the boil over a medium heat. Remove from the heat and cover the pan with a lid, then set it aside for 1 hour to infuse.

Strain the cream through a fine sieve into a measuring jug, pressing the teabags with a spoon to push through all the cream. Add more cream, if needed, to top it up to 150ml (¼ pint). Continue as for the Salted Butter Caramels (above), from the beginning but omitting the salt.

MAKES 30

100g (3½oz) unsalted butter, diced, plus extra for greasing
150ml (¼ pint) passion fruit purée (approx. 10 fruit)
300g (10½oz) caster sugar

PASSION FRUIT CARAMELS

Halve the passion fruit and scrape out the seeds and flesh into a sieve over a small bowl. Push the flesh and juice through the sieve and measure out 150ml (¼ pint) of this purée. Lightly grease a 23 × 13cm (9 × 5in) loaf tin (although the exact size is not crucial) and line with foil or baking parchment, then grease the lining. Have this ready by the hob, so that it is right by you when the caramel reaches the correct temperature.

Put all the ingredients in a heavy-based pan over a medium heat. Cook until the sugar and butter have melted, then cook the mixture, without stirring, until it reaches 122°C (252°F). Immediately remove the pan from the heat and pour the caramel into the prepared loaf tin. Leave to set for at least 4 hours before cutting into pieces. Store as for the recipes above.

Earl Grey Truffles

In the tradition of French artisans, pâtissierie and chocolate are normally viewed as very separate disciplines, but these days most modern pâtissieries carry at least a small range of chocolates. This basic milk chocolate ganache can be the foundation for many different flavours. I have flavoured mine with Earl Grey tea, a beautiful and simple pairing. To give the chocolates a more rounded flavour they are coated in dark chocolate and decorated with dried cornflowers, which are often found in loose Earl Grey tea.

MAKES ABOUT 20

FOR THE GANACHE
200g (7oz) milk chocolate (40 per cent cocoa solids), finely chopped
125ml (4fl oz) whipping cream
20g (¾oz) unsalted butter
2 teaspoons Earl Grey leaves (approx. 1 teabag)

FOR THE COATING
500g (1lb 2oz) dark chocolate (60–70 per cent cocoa solids), tempered (see page 186 and Tips)
dried cornflowers (optional)

Put the milk chocolate in a medium heatproof bowl and set aside. Put the cream in a small pan and add the butter and tea leaves, then bring them to the boil over a medium heat. Remove the pan from the heat, cover with a lid and allow the cream to infuse for 30 minutes.

Once the cream has infused, return the pan to the heat and bring the mixture back to the boil. Pour the cream through a fine sieve over the chocolate, pressing on the tea leaves to squeeze out all the cream. Leave for a few minutes before stirring together to form a silky-smooth ganache. Press a piece of clingfilm onto the surface of the ganache and chill until firm – this is best done overnight.

Line a baking tray with baking parchment. Use a teaspoon to scoop out small amounts of set ganache and quickly roll them into balls. This is best done between your fingers (rather than your palms), as they are the coolest parts of your hands. Put the rolled truffles onto the prepared baking tray and chill for 1 hour or until firm.

To coat the chocolates, put the tempered chocolate in a bowl. Drop the ganache balls, one at a time, into the tempered chocolate. Using a chocolate-dipping fork or a regular fork, lift the balls out, tapping the fork against the side of the bowl to allow the excess to drip back into the bowl. Put the truffles back on the parchment-lined baking tray and decorate with dried cornflowers, if using.

Because you have tempered the chocolate, these truffles will keep for up to a week. Store in an airtight container in a cool place away from direct sunlight.

TIPS
* Flavourings: infusing the cream with tea gives the flavour to these truffles, but you could happily replace the tea with many different flavours including all kinds of spices – cinnamon and star anise would both work wonderfully.

* Chocolate: you will have some leftover tempered chocolate, but it is easier to coat with more chocolate than needed. The leftovers can be poured into a chocolate mould or a plastic container and, once they have fully set, used again for any other recipe, reheated as described on page 186.

Palet D'or

This style of chocolate truffle was made famous by Bernachon, an acclaimed bean-to-bar chocolaterie in Lyon, but has now become a staple at chocolate shops across France. Palet d'or translates as 'golden puck', which makes sense as they are discs of ganache coated in tempered chocolate and decorated with flecks of gold leaf.

MAKES 40

FOR THE GANACHE
300g (10½oz) dark chocolate (60–70 per cent cocoa solids), finely chopped
250ml (9fl oz) whipping cream
30g (1oz) light brown sugar
20g (¾oz) unsalted butter

FOR THE DECORATION
500g (1lb 2oz) dark chocolate (60–70 per cent cocoa solids), tempered (see page 186)
acetate sheets, cut into 40 × 4cm (1½in) squares (see Resources, page 188)
1 sheet of edible gold leaf (see Resources, page 188)

To make the ganache, put the chocolate in a heatproof bowl and set aside. Put the cream in a small pan and add the sugar and butter. Bring to the boil over a medium heat, then remove from the heat and pour it over the chocolate. Leave for 2 minutes, then stir together to form a silky-smooth ganache. Leave the ganache to set for 1 hour or until it is thick enough to hold its shape.

Line two baking trays with baking parchment and transfer the ganache to a piping bag fitted with a large round piping tip. Pipe rounds 2.5cm (1in) in diameter onto the prepared trays and put a second sheet of baking parchment on top. Use another baking tray to gently flatten the ganache into discs. Transfer the trays to the refrigerator for 1 hour or until the discs are firm.

Put the tempered chocolate in a bowl. Drop the ganache discs into the tempered chocolate one at a time, submerging them to coat completely. Using a chocolate-dipping fork or a regular fork, lift the discs out, tapping the fork against the side of the bowl to allow the excess to drip back into the bowl. Put the discs onto a clean sheet of baking parchment and top each with a square of acetate.

Once the chocolate on the outside has fully set, remove the acetate (which, if the chocolate was tempered correctly, will be nice and shiny) and finish by decorating with a little piece of gold leaf using a fine, clean paintbrush.

These truffles will keep for up to a week. Store in an airtight container in a cool place away from direct sunlight.

Pavé au Chocolat

Pavé means 'pavement' or 'cobblestone', and a box of these truffles really does look like its namesake, a small, cobbled street. Traditionally, these come as tiny squares, often served in a box barely bigger than a matchbox, with a little skewer to help you eat them. The small size also makes it far too easy to eat a lot! I have made these a little larger than the classic size, but you can form them into whatever size or shape you wish.

MAKES 30

175g (6oz) dark chocolate (60–70 per cent cocoa solids), finely chopped
175ml (6fl oz) whipping cream
10g (¼oz) light brown sugar
cocoa powder, for coating (see Tip)

Line a 23 × 13cm (9 × 5in) loaf tin with a large piece of clingfilm. Put the chocolate in a heatproof bowl and set aside. Put the cream and sugar in a small pan and bring to the boil. Remove from the heat and pour the cream over the chocolate. Leave for 2 minutes before stirring together to form a silky-smooth ganache. (If you find that the ganache splits, a great way to bring it back is to use a stick blender, which will emulsify the ganache brilliantly.)

Pour the ganache into the prepared loaf tin, spreading it level, then leave it to cool at room temperature for 1 hour. Transfer the ganache to the refrigerator to set completely.

To finish the truffles, remove the ganache from the tin, transfer to a chopping board and use a thin, sharp knife to cut it into cubes. Coat the cubes in a little cocoa powder, gently shaking the truffles in a fine sieve afterwards to remove the excess.

As with all ganache-based recipes, these truffles are best served at room temperature, to ensure the perfect texture, but if you are storing them for more than a few days, keep them in the refrigerator and remove them a few hours before serving. Store in an airtight container.

TIP
If you want to give these truffles a different flavour, a great way to do this is to try coating them in freeze-dried fruit powder instead of dusting with cocoa (see Resources, page 188). Passion fruit is one of my favourites.

Blood-Orange Marshmallows

Marshmallows have definitely gone through a revival in France over recent years. No longer just a sweet found in the supermarket, they have turned into a gourmet treat, made in a myriad of flavours. I have seen pâtissierie windows decorated with jars full to the brim with marshmallows in a rainbow of colours and flavours. Here I have used blood-orange juice in place of water to give the marshmallows a wonderfully natural orange flavour. If blood oranges are out of season, you can change the juice – I have used blackcurrant, lemon and raspberry, all with great success.

MAKES 50–60

FOR THE MARSHMALLOWS
oil, preferably an oil spray, for greasing
425g (15oz) caster sugar
1 tablespoon liquid glucose
275ml (9½fl oz) blood-orange juice
10 sheets of gelatine
2 large egg whites

FOR THE COATING
50g (1¾oz) icing sugar
25g (1oz) cornflour

TIP
Blood-orange juice works well in this recipe, as the juice is a similar viscosity to water. If using other fruits you may need to thin your puree with a little water (before measuring) to make sure that it doesn't burn as it boils.

To make the marshmallows, lightly grease a 23 × 33cm (9 × 13in) baking tin. Line the tin with a piece of clingfilm, making sure that it overhangs the sides. Lightly grease the clingfilm. Put the ingredients for the coating in a small bowl and mix together, then dust the inside of the tin with this mix, setting the leftover coating aside for later.

Put the sugar, glucose and 125ml (4fl oz) of the orange juice in a large pan and bring to the boil over a medium-high heat. Cook, without stirring, until the syrup registers 121°C (250°F) on an instant-read thermometer. Meanwhile, put the remaining orange juice in a small bowl with the gelatine sheets and set aside to soften.

Put the egg whites in a clean, grease-free bowl (this is best done using a freestanding electric mixer). When the syrup reaches 110°C (230°F), whisk the whites on high speed until they hold soft peaks. Leave the syrup to continue heating to 121°C (250°F), then remove from the heat and, with the mixer still running, pour the syrup in a slow stream down the side of the bowl containing the whites, avoiding the beaters.

Put the orange and gelatine mixture in the empty pan over a medium heat, stirring until the gelatine has melted. Pour this mixture into the mixer and continue whisking the marshmallow until it is thick and has cooled down slightly, about 5–10 minutes. Scrape the marshmallow mixture into the prepared tin and, using a greased spatula, spread into an even layer. Dust the top of the marshmallow with more of the coating mixture, then set aside for 2 hours or until the marshmallow has fully set.

Turn the slab of marshmallow out onto a large chopping board and remove the clingfilm. Using a pizza cutter or kitchen scissors, cut first into long strips and then into squares. The cut edges will be sticky, so toss the marshmallows in a little more of the coating, gently shaking the marshmallows in a fine sieve to remove the excess.

The marshmallows will keep for up to a week in an airtight container.

MASTERCLASS

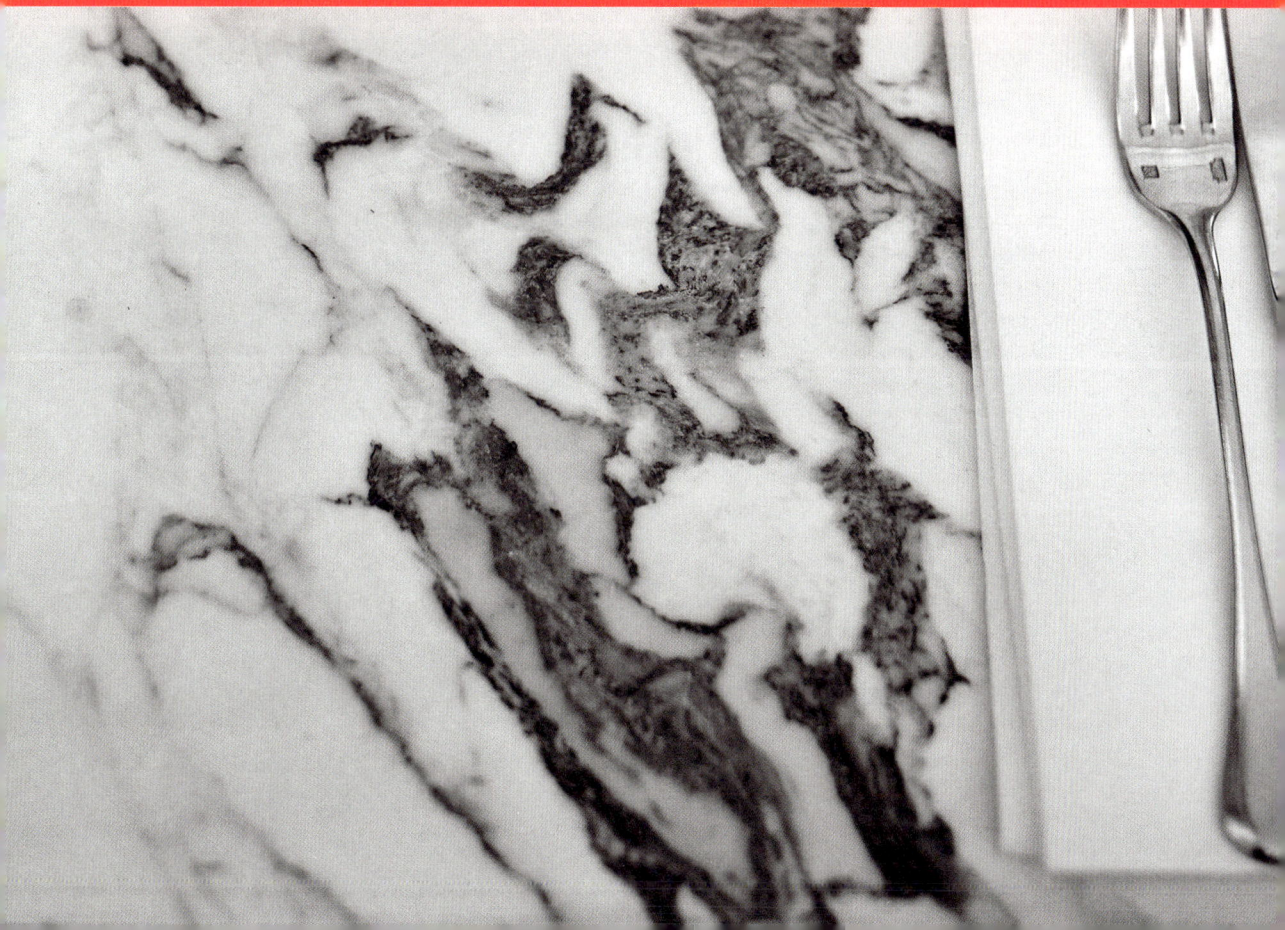

Rose, Raspberry and Lychee Cake

The combination of rose, raspberry and lychee is a modern French classic, famously invented by Pierre Hermé, one of the world's most well-regarded pastry chefs, but now used regularly by pastry chefs across France. It is a delicate blend that is so aromatic and always brings romance to my mind. This cake aims to accentuate this elegant combination of flavours.

SERVES 12

FOR THE GENOISE SPONGE

30g (1oz) unsalted butter, melted and
   slightly cooled, plus extra for greasing
5 large eggs
125g (4½oz) caster sugar
100g (3½oz) plain flour
25g (1oz) cornflour

FOR THE ROSE BUTTERCREAM

3 large egg whites
225g (8oz) caster sugar
335g (11¾oz) unsalted butter,
   at room temperature, diced
3 tablespoons rose syrup

FOR THE RASPBERRY SYRUP

125g (4½oz) caster sugar
3 tablespoons crème de framboise

FOR THE FILLING

400g (14oz) canned lychees, drained
400g (14oz) raspberries

FOR THE DECORATION

1 batch of pink Macarons (see page 176)
20–30 edible rose petals (not treated
   with pesticides)
1 large egg white, lightly whisked
caster sugar, for coating

Preheat the oven to 180°C (160°C fan/350°F), Gas Mark 4. Lightly grease a deep 23cm (9in) round cake tin, and line the base with baking parchment. For the sponge, put the eggs and sugar in a large bowl and, using an electric whisk, beat on medium speed for 5 minutes or until pale and thick; when the whisk is lifted it should form a slowly dissolving ribbon.

In a separate bowl, mix the flour and cornflour together and sift a third over the egg mixture, very gently folding together using a spatula. Repeat with the remaining two-thirds of flour mixture. Take a large spoonful of the egg mixture and add it to the butter, mixing them together until smooth. Tip this butter mixture back into the bowl with the egg mixture, and carefully fold it in to combine. Pour this sponge mixture into the prepared tin, and gently level it out. Bake for 25 minutes or until golden and coming away from the edges of the tin. Leave to cool in the tin for 10 minutes, then invert the cake onto a wire rack to cool completely.

To make the buttercream, put the egg whites and sugar in a large, clean, grease-free heatproof bowl set over a pan of gently simmering water. Whisk gently until the sugar has dissolved and the mixture is warm to the touch. Remove the bowl from the heat and, using an electric whisk, beat until the meringue is thick, glossy and cool. Add the butter, a few pieces at a time, beating until thoroughly combined and a smooth buttercream has formed. Add the rose syrup and beat to combine.

To make the syrup, put the sugar and 125ml (4fl oz) water in a pan and bring to the boil over a medium heat, then cook for 2 minutes. Remove from the heat and pour in the crème de framboise. Leave to cool slightly.

To assemble the cake, use a long, serrated knife to slice the cake into three even layers. Put one of the discs of sponge onto a serving plate and brush liberally with the raspberry syrup. Top with one-third of the buttercream, smoothing it into an even layer. Top with half the lychees and just under half the raspberries, then repeat with the second layer. Top the cake with the final layer of sponge and spread the remaining buttercream across the sides and top of the cake. Press the macarons onto the side in two rows, using the buttercream to secure them.

To crystallize the rose petals, line a baking tray with baking parchment. Brush the petals with a thin layer of egg white, then dip them into caster sugar and put them onto the prepared tray. Leave to dry out for 4 hours or until crisp. To decorate, top the cake with the remaining raspberries and the rose petals. This cake will keep for up to two days in an airtight container.

TIP

If making the macarons for this recipe ahead of time, they can be frozen for up to a month. The buttercream can be stored in an airtight container in the refrigerator for up to a week; allow it to come to room temperature, then beat it until light and fluffy before use.

Gâteau Opéra

The gâteau opéra is one of the classics of French baking and, to my mind, is one of the most elegant cakes around. It has layers of soft and moist almond sponge sandwiched together with a smooth and silky coffee-flavoured buttercream and a rich chocolate ganache. Although it is viewed as a classic, it's actually a relatively modern creation, in French-baking terms at least, having only been created in 1955 by Pâtisserie Dalloyau, which still makes my favourite version in Paris.

SERVES 10

FOR THE JOCONDE ALMOND SPONGE
25g (1oz) unsalted butter, melted, plus extra for greasing
3 large eggs
115g (4oz) ground almonds
115g (4oz) icing sugar
30g (1oz) plain flour
3 large egg whites
30g (1oz) caster sugar

FOR THE COFFEE SYRUP (SEE TIPS, OVERLEAF)
150g (5½oz) caster sugar
3 teaspoons instant espresso powder

FOR THE COFFEE BUTTERCREAM
1 tablespoon instant espresso powder
60g (2¼oz) caster sugar
3 large egg yolks
150g (5½oz) unsalted butter, at room temperature, diced

FOR THE CHOCOLATE GANACHE
50g (1¾oz) milk chocolate (35–40 per cent cocoa solids), finely chopped
50g (1¾oz) dark chocolate (60–70 per cent cocoa solids), finely chopped
4 tablespoons whipping cream
15g (½oz) unsalted butter

FOR THE CHOCOLATE GLAZE
65g (2¼oz) dark chocolate (60–70 per cent cocoa solids), finely chopped
50g (1¾oz) unsalted butter
2 tablespoons golden syrup or clear honey
55ml (2fl oz) double cream

Preheat the oven to 180°C (160°C fan/350F), Gas Mark 4. Grease two 33 × 23cm (13 × 9in) baking trays, then line with baking parchment and grease the parchment. To make the sponge, put the whole eggs, almonds and icing sugar in a large bowl and, using an electric whisk, beat for 5 minutes or until pale and thick. Sift over the flour and fold together gently using a spatula. Drizzle over the melted butter and fold to combine.

Put the egg whites in a clean, grease-free bowl and, using an electric mixer, whisk until foamy. Continue to whisk while you slowly pour in the sugar until the meringue holds soft peaks. Working in thirds, add the meringue to the egg mixture, folding together gently to combine.

Divide the batter, by weight, between the two prepared trays, and very gently level it out. Bake for 8–10 minutes until light golden brown. Remove from the oven and immediately remove the sponges from the trays. Put them onto a wire rack to cool. While the sponges are still warm, trim off the edges, because they will become crisp as they cool.

To make the coffee syrup, put the sugar and 150ml (¼ pint) water in a small pan over a medium-high heat and bring to the boil, then simmer for 5 minutes or until slightly reduced. Remove from the heat and add the espresso powder, whisking until smooth. Set aside.

To make the buttercream, put the espresso powder in a small bowl and add 2 teaspoons of boiling water, mixing to a paste. Set aside. Put the sugar and 2 tablespoons of water in a small pan over a medium heat and cook until it reaches 121°C (250°F) on an instant-read thermometer. Meanwhile, put the yolks in a bowl and, using an electric whisk, beat until pale and thickened (this is best done using a freestanding electric mixer). When the syrup is at temperature, slowly pour it into the egg yolks, whisking constantly. Continue whisking until the egg mixture has cooled to room temperature. Add the butter a few pieces at a time, beating until fully combined, before adding more to make a silky-smooth buttercream. Add the espresso mixture and beat to combine.

To make the ganache, put both types of chocolate in a small heatproof bowl and set aside. Put the cream and butter in a small pan and bring to the boil over a medium heat. Remove from the heat and pour it over the chocolate. Leave for 2 minutes, then stir together until smooth. Set aside until thickened slightly and easy to spread.

CONTINUED FROM PREVIOUS PAGE

To assemble, remove the parchment from the cakes and cut each sponge in half and put one half onto a serving plate. Brush liberally with the coffee syrup. Top with just under half the buttercream and gently smooth out to make a flat surface. Put a second sponge on top, brush with coffee syrup and spread the ganache evenly over. Add the third sponge, brush with coffee syrup and spread over a layer of buttercream, leaving enough remaining to lightly cover the top of the cake. Finish by putting the final sponge on top, brushing again with the syrup, and spreading the small remaining amount of buttercream over the top in a smooth layer. Transfer the cake to the refrigerator for 2 hours or until the buttercream is firm.

When the cake has chilled, make the chocolate glaze. Put the chocolate, butter, golden syrup and cream in a heatproof bowl set over a pan of gently simmering water, making sure the base of the bowl doesn't touch the water. Heat slowly until melted and smooth, stirring occasionally. Remove from the heat and leave to cool slightly. Pour the glaze over the cake, smoothing it out to cover the entire top of the cake. Return the cake to the refrigerator to set. Using a sharp knife, trim off the edges leaving you with clean edges.

This cake will keep for up to a week in an airtight container in the refrigerator. Bring to room temperature before serving. The coffee extract will keep in the refrigerator for two months stored in a sterilized jar.

TIPS

* There are commercial coffee extracts available, including a French brand called Trablit, but outside France it is prohibitively expensive, so making your own syrup will save you money.

* You can make the syrup in larger batches, but if keeping for more than a few days, make with a simple syrup in place of the water.

Matcha, Black Sesame and White Chocolate Cake

This recipe is based on the gâteau opéra (pages 132–134) but is given a complete makeover to give it a modern spin. The flavourings here are inspired by the Japanese influence seen in today's pâtisseries. French baking as a style is very popular in Japan, with many French pâtissiers opening shops there. The influence also travels the other way, with Japanese flavours now a common sight on pâtisseries' counters.

SERVES 10

FOR THE MATCHA JOCONDE SPONGE

25g (1oz) unsalted butter, melted, plus extra for greasing
3 large eggs
110g (3¾oz) ground almonds
115g (4oz) icing sugar
3 teaspoons matcha powder (see Resources, page 188)
30g (1oz) plain flour
3 large egg whites
30g (1oz) caster sugar

FOR THE SYRUP

75g (2½oz) caster sugar

FOR THE FRENCH BUTTERCREAM

100g (3½oz) white chocolate, finely chopped
1½ teaspoons roasted black sesame seeds
120g (4¼oz) caster sugar
4 large egg yolks
300g (10½oz) unsalted butter, at room temperature, diced
zest of 2 lemons
½ teaspoon lemon extract (optional)

FOR THE GLAZE

225g (8oz) white chocolate, finely chopped
100ml (3½fl oz) whipping cream

FOR THE DECORATION

150g (5½oz) white chocolate, finely chopped

Preheat the oven to 180°C (160°C fan/350°F), Gas Mark 4. Grease and line two 33 × 23cm (13 × 9in) baking trays and grease the baking parchment. To make the sponge, put the whole eggs, almonds, icing sugar and matcha powder in a large bowl and, using an electric whisk, beat together for 5 minutes or until pale and thick. Sift over the flour and gently fold together using a spatula. Drizzle over the melted butter and fold together.

Put the egg whites in a clean, grease-free bowl and, using an electric mixer, whisk until foamy. Continue to whisk while you slowly pour in the sugar until this meringue holds soft peaks. Add one-third of the meringue to the egg mixture and fold together, then add the remaining meringue and gently fold together until fully combined.

Divide the batter, by weight, between the two prepared trays and very gently level the mixture out. Bake for 8–10 minutes until lightly golden brown around the edges, being very careful not to over-bake. Remove from the oven and immediately remove the sponges from the trays and put them on a wire rack to cool. While the sponges are still warm, trim off the edges, as these will crisp up slightly as they cool.

To make the syrup, put the sugar and 75ml (2½fl oz) water in a small pan over a medium-high heat and bring to the boil, then cook for a few minutes or until reduced slightly. Remove from the heat and set aside.

To make the buttercream, melt the chocolate in a small heatproof bowl over a pan of gently simmering water, making sure the base of the bowl doesn't touch the water, and stirring occasionally. Leave to cool. Finely grind the black sesame seeds in a pestle and mortar and set aside.

Put the sugar and 4 tablespoons of water in a small pan over a medium heat. When the sugar has dissolved, cook until the syrup reaches 121°C (250°F) on an instant-read thermometer. Meanwhile, put the egg yolks in the bowl of an electric mixer fitted with the whisk attachment and whisk until pale and thickened (this is best done using a freestanding electric mixer). When the syrup is at temperature, and with the mixer still running, slowly pour it into the egg yolks, whisking constantly. Continue whisking until the egg mixture has cooled to room temperature. Add the butter, a few pieces at a time, beating until you have a silky-smooth buttercream. Mix in the cooled white chocolate and then divide into two bowls, one with three-quarters and one with a quarter of the buttercream.

CONTINUED FROM PAGE 135

Add the lemon zest and lemon extract, if using, to the larger quantity and the ground sesame seeds to the smaller amount, beating both until fully combined.

To assemble the cake, remove the parchment from the cakes and cut each sponge into two equal pieces. Put the first sponge layer onto a parchment-lined baking tray and brush liberally with the syrup. Top with a third of the lemon buttercream and spread into an even layer. Put the second sponge layer on top and brush liberally with the syrup, then spread over all of the black sesame buttercream in an even layer. Repeat this again, adding another third of the lemon buttercream. Finish by putting the last layer of cake on top. Brush once more with the syrup and then spread the remaining lemon buttercream over the sides and top of the cake, making the finish as neat as possible. Put the cake and the tray into the freezer and chill for at least 3 hours or until very firm.

To make the glaze, put the chocolate in a medium heatproof bowl and put the cream in a small pan and bring to the boil over a medium heat. Pour the cream over the chocolate and leave for 2 minutes before stirring to create a smooth glaze. Leave the glaze to cool for a few minutes more or until warm but not hot, while still pourable. Remove the cake from the freezer, transfer it to a wire rack and set this over a baking tray. Pour the glaze over the cake, making sure that it covers all the sides. Using two spatulas, carefully lift the cake from the rack and put it onto a serving plate. Transfer the cake to the refrigerator for 2–3 hours to thaw.

You can serve the cake as it is, but I prefer to finish it with a little chocolate decoration. If you are making the cake in advance, it is best if you temper the chocolate first (see page 186) but if you are making it to serve straightaway, there is no need to do this. Put the chocolate in a heatproof bowl over a pan of gently simmering water, making sure the base of the bowl doesn't touch the water, and stirring occasionally. Once about three-quarters of the chocolate has melted, remove the bowl from the heat and stir until all the chocolate has completely melted.

Cut out strips of baking parchment about 5cm (2in) wide. Spoon small rounds of chocolate onto the strips and, using a spatula or the back of a spoon, spread the chocolate into a teardrop shape. While the chocolate is still melted, put the strips around the edge of a rimmed baking tray so that the chocolate curves. Transfer the baking tray to the refrigerator until the chocolate has set completely. Carefully peel the decorations from the parchment and press gently around the sides of the cake.

This cake will keep for up to three days stored in the refrigerator. The French buttercream can be made up to three days in advance and stored in the refrigerator. Bring to room temperature before using it.

Gâteau St Honoré

This is, for me, one of the most beautiful French recipes. Shiny caramel-topped choux buns surrounding waves of vanilla-infused cream – a recipe that is all about textures. It uses puff and choux pastry, topped with a layer of crème pâtissière and, in my version, it is finished with a simple crème Chantilly. There is the crunch from the caramel, the crispiness from the two pastries and the smooth, rich fillings. Such an elegant and refined dish – it's no wonder it became a classic.

SERVES 10–12

FOR THE CRÈME PÂTISSIÈRE
½ vanilla pod or 1 teaspoon vanilla
   bean paste
250ml (9fl oz) whole milk
1 large egg
2 egg yolks
100g (3½oz) caster sugar
25g (1oz) cornflour

FOR THE PASTRY
250g (9oz) puff pastry (Rough Puff
   Pastry, see page 162, or store-
   bought), thawed if frozen
flour, for dusting
Pâte à Choux (see page 156)
1 large egg, beaten

FOR THE CARAMEL TOPPING
250g (9oz) caster sugar

FOR THE CRÈME CHANTILLY
300ml (½ pint) whipping cream
1 tablespoon caster sugar
1 teaspoon vanilla extract

Preheat the oven to 180°C (160°C fan/350°F), Gas Mark 4 and line two baking trays with baking parchment. To make the crème pâtissière, cut the vanilla pod, if using, in half and scrape out the seeds. Put the seeds or vanilla bean paste in a large pan and pour in the milk. Put the pan over a medium-high heat and bring to the boil.

Meanwhile, put the egg and yolks in a heatproof bowl and add the sugar and cornflour, then whisk until smooth. Pour the boiling milk over, whisking constantly to combine. Pour this mixture back into the pan, return to a medium heat, and whisk constantly until thickened, cooking for a few minutes extra to remove the taste of the cornflour. Pour this custard into a clean bowl, then press a piece of clingfilm onto the surface and put it in the refrigerator until needed.

Roll out the puff pastry on a lightly floured surface until it is about 2–3mm (¹⁄₁₆–¹⁄₈in) thick. Cut out a 23cm (9in) disc and put it onto one of the prepared baking trays. Put it in the refrigerator while you make the pâte à choux (see page 156 for instructions).

Put the choux pastry into a piping bag fitted with a 1cm (½in) plain round piping tip. Remove the puff pastry from the refrigerator and prick it all over with a fork. Pipe two circles of choux pastry onto the puff pastry, one 2cm (¾in) in from the outside edge and a second halfway towards the centre of the pastry. On the second prepared baking tray, use the remaining choux pastry to pipe 2.5cm (1in)-wide buns. Lightly brush the beaten egg all over the choux pastry. Bake for 35–40 minutes until the choux is crisp and the puff pastry is golden brown. Turn off the oven and allow the pastry to cool in the oven for 15 minutes, then transfer to a wire rack to cool completely.

When you are ready to assemble, transfer the crème pâtissière to a piping bag fitted with a small plain piping tip and use a small, sharp knife to pierce a hole in the base of each choux bun. Pipe the custard into each bun, and then spread the remaining custard across the base.

Line a baking tray with baking parchment. To make the caramel, put the sugar and 50ml (2fl oz) water in a small pan over a medium-high heat and cook, without stirring, until the sugar has dissolved and the syrup has turned a light golden brown. (Be careful that it doesn't cook too far as it can burn easily.) Remove from the heat and leave to cool for a few minutes, during which time it will colour further and thicken slightly.

CONTINUED FROM PREVIOUS PAGE

Once the caramel is a little more viscous, carefully dip the top of each choux bun into the caramel, allowing the excess to drip back into the pan. Carefully set the buns, caramel-side up, onto the prepared baking tray and leave to cool. (If you want to give your caramel a more professional look, set the choux buns, caramel-side down, inside small silicone dome moulds, which gives the caramel a more pleasing, rounded finish.) If at any point the caramel gets too thick to dip, return the pan to a medium heat until it returns to the correct texture. Once all the buns have been coated, dip the bases back into the caramel and stick the buns around the outside of the pastry base.

To make the crème Chantilly, put the cream, sugar and vanilla extract in a bowl and whisk together until the cream holds soft peaks. To achieve the finish in the picture, I have put the cream into a piping bag fitted with a St Honoré piping tip, piping in a side-to-side motion to create the wave effect. The piping tube isn't always easy to find (see Resources, page 188), but you can use a large teardrop piping tube to achieve a similar effect. You could also use a star piping tip and pipe the cream in rosettes, or simply pipe the cream into rounds using a plain round tip.

The cake is best served on the day it is assembled, but you can make the crème pâtissière and the puff pastry (if making it yourself) a couple of days in advance.

Croquembouche

The croquembouche is the classic French wedding cake normally made into a tall, towering structure that requires an expensive metal cone to assemble. To get around this, and to make the recipe more approachable and easier, I have used a large Pyrex bowl as the mould instead. This way you need to make fewer choux buns and it is easier to construct, but it also gives the cake a great modern look, which makes it perfect for all kinds of occasions, not just weddings.

SERVES 10

FOR THE CRÈME PÂTISSIÈRE FILLING

½ vanilla bean or 1 teaspoon vanilla bean paste
250ml (9fl oz) whole milk
1 large egg
2 large egg yolks
100g (3½oz) caster sugar
25g (1oz) cornflour

FOR THE CHOUX PASTRY

60g (2¼oz) unsalted butter, cut into small pieces
½ teaspoon salt
1 teaspoon caster sugar
85g (3oz) plain flour
2–3 large eggs

FOR THE CARAMEL TOPPING

400g (14oz) caster sugar

FOR THE DECORATION

200g (7oz) caster sugar
sugared almonds or edible flowers, such as pansies or violas (optional)

Preheat the oven to 180°C (160°C fan/350°F), Gas Mark 4 and line two baking trays with baking parchment. To make the crème pâtissière, cut the vanilla pod, if using, in half and scrape out the seeds. Put the seeds or vanilla bean paste in a large pan and pour in the milk. Put the pan over a medium-high heat and bring to the boil.

Meanwhile, put the egg and yolks in a heatproof bowl and add the sugar and cornflour, then whisk until smooth. Pour the boiling milk over, whisking constantly to combine. Pour this mixture back into the pan, return to a medium heat, and whisk constantly until thickened, cooking for a few minutes extra to remove the taste of the cornflour. Pour this custard into a clean bowl, then press a piece of clingfilm onto the surface. Leave to cool then put it in the refrigerator until needed.

To make the choux pastry, put the butter, salt, sugar and 120ml (4fl oz) water in a large pan over a medium-high heat. Once the butter has melted and the mixture is at a rolling boil, add the flour and immediately stir together with a wooden spoon to form a rough paste. With the pan still on the heat, beat vigorously for 2 minutes, then tip the dough into a bowl and beat for a few minutes more until it stops steaming.

Add two eggs, one at a time, and beat until fully absorbed. Check the consistency of the dough by seeing how the dough falls from the spatula. If it falls easily, forming a V-shaped ribbon, the dough is ready, but if the dough sticks to the spatula or is too thick, add the third egg, little by little, until the dough reaches the correct texture.

Transfer the dough to a piping bag fitted with a 1cm (½in) plain round piping tip and pipe the dough into 2.5cm (1in) buns on the prepared baking trays, leaving a 3cm (1¼in) space between each bun. Bake for 25–30 minutes or until golden brown. Turn off the oven and leave the choux buns to cool in the oven for 30 minutes.

When you are ready to assemble the cake, transfer the crème pâtissière to a piping bag fitted with a small plain round piping tip and use a small sharp knife to pierce a hole in the base of each choux bun. Pipe the custard into each bun and set them aside while you make the caramel topping.

CONTINUED FROM PREVIOUS PAGE

Have a 24cm (9½in)/3-litre (5¼-pint) glass or Pyrex bowl ready and a parchment-lined baking tray next to your hob. Put the sugar for the caramel topping and 250ml (9fl oz) water in a small pan over a medium-high heat and cook, without stirring, until the sugar has dissolved and the syrup has turned a light golden brown. (Be careful that it doesn't cook too far as it can burn easily.) Remove from the heat and leave to cool for a few minutes, during which time it will colour further and thicken slightly.

Once the caramel is a little more viscous, carefully dip the top of each choux bun into the caramel, allowing the excess to drip back into the pan. Carefully set the buns, caramel-side up onto the baking tray and leave to cool. (If you want to give your caramel a little more of a professional look, you can set the choux buns, caramel-side down, inside small silicone dome moulds, which will give the caramel a more pleasing rounded finish.) If at any point the caramel gets too thick to dip, put the pan back over a medium heat and cook until it returns to the correct texture.

Once all the buns have been coated, dip one bun back into the caramel to add a small amount to one side. Put this bun into the bowl and repeat with the remaining buns, using the fresh caramel to stick the buns together. Once the bowl has been fully lined with choux buns, set aside for 30 minutes so that the caramel can set completely (do not put the bowl in the refrigerator, or the caramel will become very sticky).

Carefully turn the cake out onto a serving plate – it should release from the bowl with just a little teasing. The traditional finish is spun sugar, although you could just decorate it with the almonds and flowers.

To make the spun sugar, first prepare your workspace. Put some newspaper on the floor to catch any drips, and secure three skewers, or chopsticks or even pan handles, so that they overhang the work surface and are above the newspaper. Put the sugar and 125ml (4fl oz) water in a small pan over a medium-high heat and cook, without stirring, until the sugar has dissolved and the syrup has turned a light golden brown. Remove from the heat and leave to cool for 2 minutes or until the sugar has just thickened slightly.

TIP

If you have leftover caramel that has hardened in the pan, the best way to clean it is to add water and cook until the sugar dissolves into the water.

Hold the pan with one hand and, with the other, dip a fork into the caramel and stir it to coat. Working quickly, flick the fork back and forth over the skewers. The caramel should form fine threads that land on the skewers. If the caramel is sticking to the fork or is forming very thick threads, gently reheat the caramel to thin it a little. Once you have enough spun sugar, carefully remove it from the skewers and use it to decorate the cake. This caramel is very delicate and melts very easily in warm or humid environments, so it is best made as close to serving as possible. You can then decorate the cake with any light additions, such as sugared almonds or edible flowers.

Chocolate, Caramel and Hazelnut Tarts

High-end pastry is, in many ways, about layering: with flavours as well as the physical layering of elements within a recipe. If you have ever cut into a tart or cake from a top-quality pâtisserie, you can't help but be impressed by the precision of the elements hidden inside. You can see why pastry chefs train for so many years. This tart is a simple example of this idea of layering: within the tart there are many flavours and textures that, when eaten together, create the wonderful rich flavour of cocoa and hazelnuts.

MAKES 6

FOR THE CHOCOLATE CHANTILLY
50g (1¾oz) dark chocolate (60 per cent cocoa solids), finely chopped
150ml (¼ pint) whipping cream, plus extra, or some milk, if needed
cocoa powder, for dusting

FOR THE PASTRY
½ recipe Pâte Sucrée (see page 158), chilled

FOR THE HAZELNUT CARAMEL LAYER
125g (4½oz) hazelnuts, roughly chopped
Salted Caramel Sauce (see page 185)

FOR THE CRUNCH LAYER
70g (2½oz) waffle cones or feuilletine
2 tablespoons cacao nibs (optional)
80g (2¾oz) milk chocolate (30–40 per cent cocoa solids), finely chopped

Preheat the oven to 180°C (160°C fan/350°F), Gas Mark 4 and line a baking tray with baking parchment. To make the chocolate Chantilly, put the chocolate in a large heatproof bowl and set aside. Put the cream in a medium pan and bring to the boil over a medium heat. Pour it over the chocolate and leave for 2 minutes, then stir together until you have a smooth chocolate mixture. Press a sheet of clingfilm onto the surface, then put it in the refrigerator for 2–3 hours until completely chilled.

To make the tart shells, line six individual 8cm (3¼in) tart rings or moulds with the pastry according to the instructions on page 164, then put in the refrigerator for 30 minutes or until firm. Line the tarts with baking parchment and fill with baking beans or rice. Bake for 15 minutes, then remove the parchment and beans and bake for a further 10 minutes or until the pastry is golden. Set aside and leave to cool.

To make the hazelnut layer, put the hazelnuts on a baking tray and toast in the preheated oven for 10 minutes. Leave to cool. If the salted caramel sauce is chilled, reheat it slightly in a pan over a low heat to make it more fluid. Stir the chopped hazelnuts into the sauce. Divide this mixture among the tart shells, then chill them in the refrigerator until the caramel sets.

To make the crunch layer, if using the waffle cones, use a rolling pin to crush them into small pieces. Put the feuilletine or crushed cones in a medium bowl and add the cacao nibs, if using. Set aside. Melt the chocolate in a heatproof bowl over a pan of gently simmering water, making sure the base of the bowl doesn't touch the water, stirring occasionally. Add the chocolate to the feuilletine and mix together until fully coated. Divide this mixture between the tarts, spreading it carefully into an even layer. Return to the refrigerator for 1 hour until the chocolate has set.

To assemble the tarts, remove the tarts from the refrigerator and allow them to come to room temperature. Remove the chilled chocolate Chantilly mixture from the refrigerator and whisk until it forms soft peaks. (Because of the chocolate, it will whip very quickly, so watch carefully; if you do over-whip it, stir in a little milk or cream to loosen it). Transfer the Chantilly to a piping bag fitted with a 5mm (¼in) plain piping tip and pipe the cream on top of the tarts in a spiral. Dust with a little cocoa powder before serving. If not serving immediately, store the tarts in an airtight container in the refrigerator for up to two days. Bring to room temperature before serving.

Caramelized White Chocolate, Ginger Caramel and Macadamia Tarts

White chocolate gets a bad rap – it's not even considered real chocolate by a lot of people and is criticized as being overly sweet with little flavour. If you are one of these people, this recipe might just change your mind. By slowly caramelizing the chocolate in the oven, it takes on a wonderful flavour, reminiscent of dulce de leche, and it is beautiful when paired with the pears and ginger in this recipe. When you first look at this recipe it might seem daunting (it is probably the longest recipe I have ever written), but please believe me when I say that it is definitely achievable. It just takes a little time and effort, but that effort is so worthwhile, as this is certainly a dish with the wow! factor.

MAKES 8

½ recipe Pâte Sucrée (see page 158), chilled

FOR THE GINGER MACADAMIA CARAMEL

300g (10½oz) macadamia nuts, roughly chopped
160ml (5½fl oz) whipping cream
5cm (2in) piece of fresh root ginger, peeled and sliced
200g (7oz) caster sugar
15g (½oz) unsalted butter

FOR THE CARAMELIZED PEARS

15g (½oz) unsalted butter
15g (½oz) light brown sugar
2 large Conference pears, peeled, cored and diced

FOR THE CARAMELIZED WHITE CHOCOLATE BAVAROIS

225ml (8fl oz) whole milk
4 large egg yolks
75g (2½oz) caster sugar
3 sheets of leaf gelatine
150g (5½oz) Caramelized White Chocolate, melted (see page 182)
225ml (8fl oz) whipping cream

FOR THE CARAMELIZED WHITE CHOCOLATE GLAZE

225g (8oz) Caramelized White Chocolate (see page 182)
140ml (4½fl oz) whipping cream

Preheat the oven to 180°C (160°C fan/350°F), Gas Mark 4 and line a baking tray with baking parchment. To make the tart shells, line eight individual 8cm (3¼in) tart rings or moulds with pâte sucrée according to the instructions on page 164. To line all eight you will need to re-roll the leftover scraps of pastry. Put them in the refrigerator for 30 minutes or until firm. Line the tarts with baking parchment or a double layer of clingfilm and fill with baking beans or rice. Bake for 15 minutes, then remove the parchment and the beans and bake for a further 10 minutes or until the pastry is golden. Leave to cool.

Put the macadamia nuts onto a baking tray and toast in the preheated oven for 10 minutes or until fragrant. Leave to cool.

To make the caramelized pears, melt the butter and sugar in a medium frying pan over a medium heat. Cook for 5 minutes until the mixture is bubbling, add the pears and cook, stirring occasionally, for 5 minutes or until the pears are caramelized and softened. Tip the pear mixture into a small bowl and set aside until cool.

Divide the pear mixture between eight 7cm (2¾in) silicone dome moulds (you will need two 6-cup trays for this). Put the moulds in the freezer for 1 hour or until the pear mixture has frozen. Remove the moulds from the freezer and carefully turn out the caramelized pear pieces onto a parchment-lined baking tray and return to the freezer until needed.

To make the bavarois, put the milk in a medium pan and bring to the boil. Meanwhile, put the egg yolks and the sugar in a heatproof bowl and whisk together. Put the gelatine in a small bowl and add enough ice-cold water to cover. Once the milk has come to the boil, pour it over the egg mixture, whisking constantly. Pour this mixture into the pan, return it to the heat and cook, stirring constantly, until the custard thickens (or it reaches about 75–80°C/167–176°F on an instant-read thermometer). Pour the custard into a bowl and add the caramelized white chocolate. Squeeze out the water from the soaked gelatine and add it to the bowl, then stir until the chocolate and gelatine have melted.

Cover the bowl with clingfilm, then transfer to the refrigerator to chill until the custard has cooled and the mixture has just started to set around the sides of the bowl.

Whip the cream until it holds very soft peaks, and carefully fold this through the custard, using a spatula, until smooth and fully combined. Fill eight of the silicone dome moulds half-full with the bavarois and carefully press the frozen pear pieces into the centre. Top with the remaining bavarois and transfer the moulds to the freezer overnight until frozen solid.

To make the ginger macadamia caramel, put the cream and ginger in a small pan and bring to the boil. Remove the pan from the heat and cover with a lid. Leave the ginger to infuse in the cream for 1 hour.

Strain the cream through a fine sieve into a measuring jug, and top up the cream to 120ml (4fl oz) if needed. Put the sugar in a medium pan over a medium heat and cook, without stirring, until the sugar has melted and caramelized, turning a dark caramel. (Be careful that it doesn't cook too far as it can burn easily.) Remove the pan from the heat and carefully add half the cream – this will bubble up violently, so pour slowly. Once the bubbling has settled, stir in the remaining cream, returning the pan to the heat if any lumps have formed. Add the butter and three-quarters of the nuts, and stir to combine. Once the caramel has cooled slightly, divide it between the tart shells.

To make the glaze, put the caramelized white chocolate in a heatproof bowl and set it aside. Put the cream in a small pan and bring to the boil over a medium heat. Pour the cream over the chocolate, stirring until you have a smooth, pourable glaze.

Remove the bavarois domes from the freezer and carefully unmould them onto a wire rack set over a baking tray. Leave the glaze to cool slightly until warm, but not hot. Pour the glaze over the domes, making sure that the entire surface is covered (see Tip). Using a palette knife, lift the domes from the wire rack and carefully put them on top of the tarts. To decorate, chop the remaining nuts so that they are fairly fine, and press them around the base of the domes, where they meet the tarts.

These tarts will keep for up to three days in the refrigerator. Bring them to room temperature before serving.

TIP

The recipe for the glaze makes more than you will need, but it is easier to glaze with more than with less. The excess can be scraped off the tray and used as a sauce for ice cream or crêpes.

Chocolate Tart

The chocolate tart is a mainstay, appearing on restaurant menus and in almost every pâtisserie. You can make simple versions or turn it into something more elaborate. To bring another flavour to this recipe I have added a tonka bean-flavoured buttercream; tonka bean has a unique flavour reminiscent of vanilla and cloves, with added floral notes. It is a favourite of pastry chefs but is rarely seen, especially outside France.

SERVES 12

FOR THE PASTRY
½ recipe Pâte Sucrée
   (see page 158), chilled

FOR THE CHOCOLATE FILLING
300ml (½ pint) whipping cream
30g (1oz) unsalted butter
200g (7oz) milk chocolate (30–40 per
   cent cocoa solids), finely chopped
100g (3½oz) dark chocolate (60–70 per
   cent cocoa solids), finely chopped

**FOR THE TONKA BEAN
BUTTERCREAM**
120g (4¼oz) caster sugar
4 large egg yolks
300g (10½oz) unsalted butter, at
   room temperature, diced
1 tonka bean

FOR THE DECORATION
300g (10½oz) dark chocolate
   (60–70 per cent cocoa solids),
   tempered (see page 186)

TIP
To make the chocolate curls, pour the tempered chocolate over the back of a baking tray and spread it into a thin, even layer. Put the tray into the freezer for 2 minutes or until the chocolate has almost set. Remove the tray from the freezer and, using a flat metal edge, scrape the chocolate in a smooth motion away from yourself to create curls.

Preheat the oven to 180°C (160°C fan/350°F), Gas Mark 4 and line a baking tray with baking parchment. To make the tart shell, line a 23cm (9in) tart ring or loose-based tart tin with pâte sucrée (see page 164). Put the tart onto the baking tray and put in the refrigerator for 30 minutes or until firm.

Remove the pastry from the refrigerator and line with a piece of baking parchment, then fill with baking beans or rice. Bake for 20 minutes, then remove the parchment and the beans and bake for a further 5–10 minutes or until golden. Leave to cool to room temperature before assembling.

For the filling, put the cream and butter into a medium saucepan and bring to the boil. While the cream is coming to temperature, put both types of chocolate into a medium heatproof bowl. Once the cream is at temperature, pour over the chocolate and allow to sit for 2 minutes, before stirring together to form a silky-smooth ganache. Pour the chocolate mixture into the cooled tart shell and leave to cool and set at room temperature.

To make the buttercream, put the sugar and 3 tablespoons of water in a small pan over a medium heat and cook until it reaches 121°C (250°F) on an instant-read thermometer. Meanwhile, put the egg yolks in a bowl and, using an electric whisk, beat until pale and thickened (this is best done using a freestanding electric mixer). When the syrup is at temperature, and with the mixer still running, slowly pour the syrup into the egg yolks. Continue whisking until the egg mixture has cooled to room temperature, add the butter, a few pieces at a time, beating until fully combined before adding more. You should have a silky-smooth buttercream. Grate in about three-quarters of the tonka bean, or to taste, and beat for 2 minutes to combine.

To decorate the tart, cut out a 23cm (9in) circle of acetate, cover it with a thin layer of tempered chocolate and leave to set at room temperature for 1 hour, then put it in the refrigerator to cool for 30 minutes. Use the remaining chocolate to make chocolate curls (see Tip).

To assemble the tart, transfer the buttercream to a piping bag fitted with a 1.5cm (⅝in) plain round piping tip and pipe buttercream across the top of the tart. Put the disc of tempered chocolate on top and scatter the chocolate curls over. The tart will keep for up to three days in the refrigerator. Bring it to room temperature a few hours before serving.

Concorde

The concorde is traditionally a cake made of chocolate meringue discs layered with chocolate mousse, created by one of the godfathers of modern French pastry, Gaston Lenôtre. To put my own stamp on the recipe I have made it with a white chocolate mousse and added a pineapple compote, giving the dessert a stunning bright white finish, c'est très chic!

SERVES 12

FOR THE PINEAPPLE COMPOTE
500g (1lb 2oz) pineapple (approx.
 1 large pineapple), cored and diced
100g (3½oz) caster sugar

FOR THE MERINGUE
5 large egg whites
pinch of salt
160g (5¾oz) caster sugar
160g (5¾oz) icing sugar

FOR THE WHITE CHOCOLATE MOUSSE
150g (5½oz) white chocolate,
 finely chopped
400ml (14fl oz) whipping cream
zest of 2 limes
2 large egg whites
30g (1oz) caster sugar

Put the pineapple and sugar in a medium pan with 3 tablespoons of water. Cook over a medium heat for 15–20 minutes until the fruit is just starting to break down and the liquid has reduced to a syrup. Pour into a small bowl and put it in the refrigerator until needed.

Preheat the oven to 110°C (90°C fan/225°F), Gas Mark ¼ and line three baking trays with baking parchment. Draw three 20cm (8in) circles on the back of the sheets of parchment. To make the meringue, put the egg whites and salt in a clean, grease-free bowl and, using an electric mixer, whisk until they form soft peaks. Continue to whisk while you slowly pour in the caster sugar until the meringue is stiff and glossy. Sift over the icing sugar in two batches and gently fold together until fully combined. Transfer the meringue to a piping bag fitted with a 1.5cm (⅝in) plain round piping tip. Pipe the meringue into three discs, using your templates as a guide. Pipe the remaining meringue into long strips alongside the discs. Bake for 1 hour 40 minutes or until the meringue is crisp, turning the trays occasionally. Turn off the oven and leave the meringues to cool completely.

To make the mousse, melt the chocolate in a heatproof bowl over a pan of gently simmering water, making sure the base of the bowl doesn't touch the water, and stirring occasionally. Remove from the heat.

Put the cream and lime zest in a large bowl and whisk until just holding soft peaks. Put the egg whites in a clean, grease-free bowl and, using an electric mixer, whisk until foamy. Continue to whisk while you slowly pour in the sugar until this meringue holds soft peaks. To bring the mousse together, fold the white chocolate into the cream, then fold the meringue into the cream mixture in two additions.

To assemble the cake, put one of the meringue discs onto a plate and spread a thin layer of the mousse over the top. Spread half the pineapple compote over the mousse. Cover with another thin layer of mousse and gently press another disc on top. Repeat this layering a second time. Gently press the final meringue onto the cake and spread the remaining mousse over the top and sides.

To finish, use a serrated knife to very gently cut the strips of meringue into short pieces about 2.5cm (1in) long. Gently press the meringue pieces all over the sides and top of the cake, using the mousse to secure them. Once finished, put the cake in the freezer overnight. This will set the mousse and slightly soften the meringue, which makes it easier to cut and nicer to eat. To serve, transfer the cake to the refrigerator and leave it to thaw for a few of hours before serving chilled or at room temperature.

This keeps for up to three days in the refrigerator or for up to two weeks frozen.

CHAPTER FIVE

BASICS

Pâte à Choux (Choux Pastry)

Choux pastry may be my favourite pastry to work with. It comes together in minutes and can be used to create some of my favourite recipes, such as the Gâteau St Honoré (page 139) or the Speculoos Éclairs (page 35). It is not difficult to make, but be sure to follow the recipe carefully, as technique is very important, especially when it comes to adding the egg: too much and the pastry won't hold its shape; too little and it won't expand properly, and will be prone to tearing.

MAKES 12 ÉCLAIRS OR 20 CHOUX BUNS

60g (2¼oz) unsalted butter, diced
¼ teaspoon salt
1 teaspoon caster sugar
40g (1½oz) plain flour
45g (1½oz) strong white bread flour
2–3 large eggs

Put the butter, salt, sugar and 120ml (4fl oz) water in a medium pan over a medium-high heat. Once the butter has melted and the mixture is at a rolling boil, add the flours and quickly stir together with a wooden spoon until the mixture forms a dough.

With the pan still on the heat, stir vigorously for 2 minutes, then tip the dough into a bowl and beat for a few minutes until it stops steaming. These two actions help to cook the flour and dry out the dough, which in turn helps it to absorb more egg. This helps the choux pastry to expand properly as it bakes.

Add the eggs, one at a time, beating until fully absorbed before adding the next. Depending on the flour used and how much water evaporated as you made the dough, the choux pastry will need varying amounts of egg, so the above is given as a guide. With this recipe I usually add two eggs and then very slowly start adding the remaining egg, checking the texture of the dough after each addition. You are looking for a dough that has a shine, and when it is lifted from the bowl, it should fall from the spatula in a ribbon that forms a V-shape. If the dough doesn't contain enough egg, it won't expand properly and will be prone to cracking as it bakes; if there is too much egg, the dough won't hold its shape and will collapse as it bakes.

To prevent the dough from drying out and forming a skin, immediately put the dough into a piping bag and use according to your recipe. This dough can be chilled for a few days as long as it is covered completely (I find it easier to put it in a bowl and press a sheet of clingfilm onto the surface). It can also be frozen; however, my preference is to always make the dough when needed, it takes no time at all and I find it expands a little less when it has been chilled or frozen.

When it comes to baking, some recipes will have you start the choux at a high temperature for a few minutes before lowering and baking at a lower temperature. I find this unnecessary and get the most consistent results at 180°C (160°C fan/350°F), Gas Mark 4, which is how all my choux pastry recipes in this book are baked. To guarantee a crisp pastry, bake until the pastry is golden brown, and then turn off the oven and allow the pastry to cool in the oven for 30 minutes. This step helps the pastry to dry out completely, so that it holds it shape and stays crisp for longer.

CHOUX PASTRY BAKES TO THE SHAPE IN WHICH IT IS
PIPED SO A STEADY HAND IS CRUCIAL.

Pâte Sucrée (Sweet Pastry)

This is one of my all-time favourite doughs to work with. It has just the right level of sweetness, a great texture and tastes fantastic. Even baked into simple rounds and served as a biscuit it would taste great. It has a high ratio of fat to flour, so it needs to be kept cold when rolling out to avoid it becoming sticky. If you follow the instructions on lining tart tins on page 164, you won't have any problems.

MAKES ENOUGH FOR 2 LARGE TARTS OR 12 INDIVIDUAL TARTS

1 vanilla pod or 2 teaspoons vanilla
  bean paste
400g (14oz) plain flour, plus extra
  for dusting
35g (1¼oz) ground almonds
75g (2½oz) icing sugar
pinch of salt
250g (9oz) unsalted butter, diced
  and chilled
2 large egg yolks
approx. 1 tablespoon ice-cold water

Cut the vanilla pod, if using, in half and scrape out the seeds. Put the seeds or vanilla bean paste in the bowl of a food processor. Add flour, almonds, icing sugar and salt, and pulse to combine. Add the butter and pulse until the mixture resembles breadcrumbs. Add the egg yolks and pulse until fully combined. (Alternatively, put the flour, almonds, icing sugar, salt and vanilla in a large bowl and mix to combine. Add the butter and rub together using your fingertips, or use a pastry cutter, until the mixture resembles breadcrumbs. Add the egg yolks and mix together until the dough just starts to come together.) If the pastry isn't coming together into a uniform mass, add 1 tablespoon of ice-cold water and pulse, or mix, until the dough starts to come together. Be careful not to over-process the dough, or the finished pastry will be tough and chewy.

Turn the dough out onto a lightly floured work surface and gently knead into a smooth, uniform dough. Divide into two pieces, pressing into a flat round if making large tarts and into thick logs if making individual tarts. Wrap the pastry in clingfilm and put it in the refrigerator for at least 1 hour before using.

As with most pastry, this can be chilled and kept for up to a week before using, or it can be frozen for up to two months.

MAKES ENOUGH FOR 1 LARGE TART OR 6 INDIVIDUAL TARTS

160g (5¾oz) plain flour, plus extra
  for dusting
40g (1½oz) cocoa powder
15g (½oz) ground almonds
35g (1¼oz) icing sugar
pinch of salt
125g (4½oz) unsalted butter, diced
  and chilled
1 large egg yolk
approx. 1 tablespoon ice-cold water

SWEET CHOCOLATE PASTRY

This pastry is a wonderful variation on the classic pâte sucrée, perfect for anything where you want to add a rich cocoa flavour to your recipe. Because of the high ratio of butter and the addition of cocoa powder, it can be a little tricky to work with, so I find it best if it is rolled between sheets of baking parchment or clingfilm. This way nothing can stick to the work surface or rolling pin, and if the dough becomes sticky you can easily put it in the refrigerator to chill.

Put the flour in the bowl of a food processor and add the cocoa powder, almonds, icing sugar and salt, then pulse to combine. Add the butter and pulse until the mixture resembles breadcrumbs. Add the egg yolk and pulse until fully combined. (Alternatively, put the flour, cocoa powder, almonds, icing sugar and salt in a large bowl and mix to combine. Add the butter and rub together using your fingertips or a pastry cutter until the mixture resembles breadcrumbs. Add the egg yolk and mix together until the dough just starts to come together.)

**WORK THE PASTRY AS LITTLE AS POSSIBLE,
YOU DON'T WANT TO MELT THE BUTTER.**

If the pastry isn't coming together into a uniform mass, add 1 tablespoon of ice-cold water and pulse, or mix, until the dough starts to come together. Be careful not to over-process the dough, or you will make the pastry tough and chewy.

Turn the dough out onto a lightly floured work surface and gently knead it into a uniform dough. Press into a flat round if making a large tart and into a thick log shape if making individual tarts. Put it in the refrigerator for at least 1 hour before using.

As with most pastry, this can be wrapped in clingfilm, chilled and kept for up to a week before using, or it can be frozen for up to two months.

Pâte Brisée (Shortcrust Pastry)

Known as shortcrust pastry in English, pâte brisée is often used in more rustic dishes where a sweet, crumbly pastry isn't desired. It is great in recipes such as a Flan Parisien (page 28) or instead of puff pastry for an apple tart, where its simplicity helps the main ingredient become the star. Perhaps the most basic of pastry recipes, pâte brisée is also the easiest to work with, just be sure not to overwork the dough, because it becomes very tough. The same goes for rolling. If you want to re-roll any scraps, do this only once; the more the dough is handled the worse the finished result will be.

**MAKES ENOUGH FOR
1 LARGE TART**

225g (8oz) plain flour, plus extra
  for dusting
pinch of salt
1 tablespoon caster sugar
120g (4¼oz) unsalted butter, diced
  and chilled
2 tablespoons ice-cold water

Put the flour, salt and sugar in the bowl of a food processor and pulse to combine. Add the butter and pulse until the mixture resembles small pea-sized pieces. Add the water one tablespoon at a time, pulsing after each addition. (Alternatively, put the flour, salt and sugar in a large bowl and mix to combine. Add the butter and rub together using your fingertips or a pastry cutter until the mixture resembles coarse breadcrumbs. Add the water one tablespoon at a time and mix together.) The dough needs just enough water so that it starts coming together. If too much is added, the dough will shrink as it bakes; if not enough is added, the dough will be tricky to work with and will split when you roll it out.

Turn the dough out onto a lightly floured work surface and lightly knead until it forms a uniform dough. Press into a flat round and wrap in clingfilm. Put it in the refrigerator for at least 1 hour before using.

As with most pastry, this can be chilled and kept for up to a week before using, or it can be frozen for up to two months.

Rough Puff Pastry

Puff pastry is a magical concoction, a seemingly simple mixture of flour, salt, butter and water, but with the correct technique it puffs up in the oven creating the flakiest of doughs. Classic puff pastry takes a little extra time and skill to make. Although it's not too difficult to make at home, many people find it a daunting task, so this recipe makes a quick and simple version that still rises and puffs up wonderfully.

MAKES 500G (1LB 2OZ)

200g (7oz) plain flour, plus extra for dusting
pinch of salt
200g (7oz) unsalted butter, chilled
  and diced into 5mm (¼in) pieces
100ml (3½fl oz) ice-cold water

Put the flour and salt in the bowl of a food processor and pulse to combine. Add the butter and pulse a couple of times (the butter is already diced small, so you are just combining it here, not really breaking it down in size). Pour in about 4 tablespoons of the water and pulse once to combine. If the dough still seems a little dry, add the remaining water and pulse again to combine. (Alternatively, put the flour and salt in a bowl and add the diced butter. Mix it in using a blunt knife to cut the pieces very slightly in size. Add 4 tablespoons of the water and stir to combine, then add the remaining water if the mixture seems dry.)

Tip the mixture onto a work surface and gently bring it together into a uniform dough – it should be soft but not sticky. Lightly flour the work surface and roll out the dough, with the short edge facing you, into a long rectangle, three times as long as it is wide, roughly 15 × 45cm (6 × 17¾in) (although the exact proportions are not crucial). Brush off any excess flour.

Fold the top third of the dough over the middle third, then fold the bottom third over the other two-thirds, as if you are folding a business letter. Turn the dough through 90 degrees so that the open ends are facing you. Repeat the rolling and folding process and then put it in the refrigerator for 30 minutes before repeating the rolling and folding twice more. Chill the dough for 1 hour before using.

Kept chilled in the refrigerator and wrapped in clingfilm, this dough will keep for up to a week, and frozen it will keep for up to two months.

MAKE SURE NOT TO PROCESS THE BUTTER TOO MUCH; IF YOU CAN'T SEE STREAKS OF BUTTER IN THE FINISHED DOUGH IT WON'T PUFF UP.

How to Line a Tart Tin

Remove the pastry from the refrigerator and, if it is too firm, leave it to soften at room temperature for 15 minutes or until pliable enough to roll. Dust a work surface and the top of the dough with a little flour.

Using a rolling pin, gently roll out the dough, turning the dough regularly. This helps to prevent the dough from sticking to the surface and it also helps to ensure a round shape and an even, flat surface.

For most tarts you will need to roll out the dough to about 2mm (1/16in) thick. With experience, you can do this by eye, but if you want to know for sure, you can use two pieces of wood of the desired thickness to act as guides. Put the guides alongside the pastry as you roll, resting your rolling pin over the guides. This will prevent the dough from becoming too thin.

If at this point your dough has warmed up and is too soft to handle, transfer it to a parchment-lined baking tray and chill it for 5–10 minutes until cold enough to handle, but not so cold that it is no longer flexible.

INDIVIDUAL TARTS Take the roll of dough from the refrigerator and cut it into discs (six for a half recipe, 12 if making the whole batch). Rolling these individual rounds of dough is easier than cutting out discs from a large piece, because it prevents the dough from warming up and it is simpler to get thin pastry this way.

TIP
If you decide to use clingfilm, make sure that you use a good-quality version as cheaper ones can melt in the oven.

TO LINE A TART TIN OR RING, put the tin onto parchment-lined baking tray beside your rolled-ou pastry. Carefully roll the pastry onto your rolling pin then lift it up and move your baking tray underneath Carefully unroll the pastry into your mould.

Lift up the overhang and gently press the dough int the corners of your tin or ring. By lifting the dough, yo will prevent it from stretching or tearing.

Once you have fully lined the ring, use the rolling pin t roll over the edge of the tart ring, to cut off the exces pastry. Gently press the dough against the sides of th tart ring to give you a smooth, thin pastry shell.

Line the pastry with a crumpled layer of bakin parchment, or a double layer of clingfilm. Fill the ta with baking beans or rice and fold the excess clingfil back over the beans or rice. Bake the tart blind accordin to the recipe.

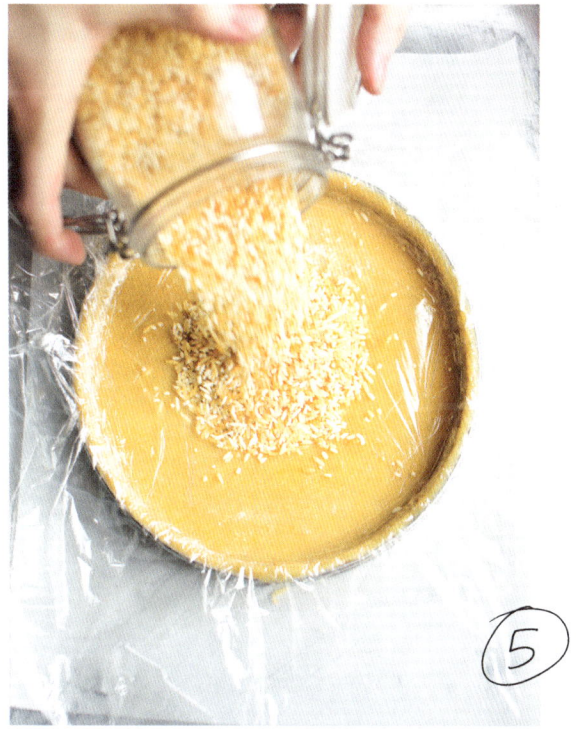

Simple Croissant Dough

Croissants may well be the most recognizable French pastry. I definitely couldn't write a book on French baking and not include them. I did, however, want to see if it is possible to bake a croissant at home that is both delicious and yet uses an easier, quicker method than the traditional one. What I have come up with is like a rough puff pastry with added yeast, which results in a wonderful homemade croissant. It is also a very useful dough to have in your repertoire – it can be used to make all kinds of Danish pastries as well as the wonderful Kouign Amann on page 42.

MAKES 8

4 tablespoons whole milk, lukewarm
4 tablespoons water, lukewarm
125g (4½oz) plain flour, plus extra
  for dusting
125g (4½oz) strong white bread flour
7g (⅛oz) fast-action dried yeast
30g (1oz) caster sugar
½ teaspoon salt
225g (8oz) unsalted butter, chilled
1 large egg, for eggwash

Put the milk and water in a medium bowl, mix to combine and set aside. Put the flours, yeast, sugar and salt in the bowl of a food processor and pulse to combine. Dice 125g (4½oz) of the butter into small pieces, about 1cm (½in) in size. Add to the food processor and pulse once or twice just to mix together. This is the most important stage: if the butter is mixed too much into the flour, the dough won't expand and puff up as it bakes, so it is better to err on the side of caution with the mixing. If you cannot see chunks of butter, you have processed the dough too much. (Alternatively, mix all the dry ingredients together in a medium bowl. Add the diced 125g/4½oz butter, as above, and very lightly rub it into the flour, or use a pastry cutter. Do this briefly just to start to combine it – as explained above, you still need to see chunks of butter.)

Tip the butter and flour mixture into the liquids and, using a spatula, fold the dry ingredients into the liquid, trying to combine everything without making the butter pieces any smaller. Once you have formed a rough dough, tip this out onto a work surface and very lightly work it into a ball of dough. Form the dough into a flat rectangle, wrap in clingfilm and put it in the refrigerator for 45 minutes. Meanwhile, put the remaining chunk of butter in the freezer to chill it thoroughly (it needs to be hard).

Lightly flour a work surface and roll out the dough away from you into a long rectangle three times as long as it is wide, about 15 × 45cm (6 × 17¾in) (although the exact measurements are not crucial). Brush off any excess flour. Take the butter out of the freezer and coarsely grate it over the bottom two-thirds of the dough. Fold the top third of the dough over the middle third, then fold the bottom third over the other two-thirds, as if folding a business letter. This is known as the first turn. Wrap the dough in clingfilm and chill in the refrigerator for 20 minutes.

Remove the dough from the refrigerator and turn the dough 90 degrees so that the open ends are facing you. Repeat the rolling and folding process twice more, giving the dough a total of three turns. Wrap the finished dough in clingfilm and put it in the refrigerator overnight before using.

At this stage the dough can be used for any of the Danish pastry recipes, and although the recipe is slightly different, it is also the same basic method for making the Kouign Amann (page 42).

CONTINUED FROM PREVIOUS PAGE

Line a baking tray with baking parchment. To form the dough into croissants, roll into a 20 × 60cm (8 × 24in) rectangle and trim off the edges, then cut out eight 12cm (4½in)-wide triangles. Gently stretch the triangles to extend the length slightly. Roll up the triangles from the wide end and shape into a classic croissant. Put the rolled croissants onto the prepared baking tray and cover with a piece of clingfilm. Leave to prove at room temperature for 2–3 hours until doubled in size.

Preheat the oven to 200°C (180°C fan/400°F), Gas Mark 6. Lightly whisk the egg with 1 teaspoon of water and use this eggwash to brush over the croissants. Bake for 20–25 minutes until a deep golden brown. Remove the tray from the oven and allow the croissants to cool on the tray for 5 minutes before transferring to a wire rack to cool completely.

Croissants are best served within a few hours of baking, but they can also be frozen for up to a month.

Brioche

The famous phrase uttered by Marie Antoinette is commonly misquoted as 'Let them eat cake' when in fact it was 'Let them eat brioche', and personally I can see why! For me it is the king of French breads: it has a beautiful buttery smell, a light texture and it is also the most versatile. It can be used in so many different recipes, from the Brioche Suisse (see page 99) to the Almond Bostock (see page 64), as well as many other uses. It is definitely a recipe worth mastering.

MAKES 2 SMALL LOAVES OR 10 ROLLS

300g (10½oz) plain flour
300g (10½oz) strong white bread flour
30g (1oz) caster sugar
2 teaspoons salt
140ml (4½fl oz) whole milk, lukewarm
14g (½oz) fast-action dried yeast
6 large eggs
250g (9oz) unsalted butter, at room temperature, diced, plus extra for greasing
pearl sugar (see Resources, page 188), to decorate (optional)

TIP
It is entirely possible to make brioche by hand, but it is a much harder job, and i would suggest making it in a freestanding electric mixer if you can. This will not only be easier and a lot quicker but it will also give you a lighter finished loaf.

To start, put the flours, sugar and salt in the bowl of an electric mixer fitted with the dough hook attachment and mix together to combine. Put the milk and yeast in a jug and mix together until the yeast has dissolved. Pour this mixture into the mixer followed by five of the eggs. Turn the mixer on to a medium-low speed and mix together until a rough dough is formed. Knead, using the mixer, for a further 10 minutes or until the dough is smooth and elastic. With the mixer still on, add the butter, a couple of pieces at a time, until fully combined. Once all the butter has been incorporated, knead the dough, again at medium-low speed, for 10–15 minutes until the dough no longer sticks to the sides of the bowl.

Put the dough in a large, lightly greased bowl and cover with clingfilm. Transfer the bowl to the refrigerator and leave to rise slowly for 8–10 hours. Next morning, remove the dough from the refrigerator and press gently to knock it back.

If making brioche loaves you will need two 23 × 13cm (9 × 5in) loaf tins. Divide the dough into four equal pieces and form these into rounds, then put two balls into each loaf tin. Cover the tins with clingfilm and leave in a warm place to prove until doubled in size; depending on the temperature of the dough and the room, this can take 2–3 hours. If making individual rolls, divide the dough into ten equal pieces and form into rounds. These can then either be put on a parchment-lined baking tray, or into individual fluted brioche moulds, or even into muffin cups. Whichever method you choose, cover the rolls with a sheet of lightly greased clingfilm and allow to prove as for the loaves.

Preheat the oven to 180°C (160°C fan/350°F), Gas Mark 4. To test the bread has proved fully, press with a lightly floured finger. If the dough springs back slowly, it is ready for the oven; if it springs back quickly, it needs a little more time to prove.

Lightly whisk the remaining egg with 1 teaspoon of water and use to brush the top of the dough, then sprinkle with a little pearl sugar, if you like. Bake the loaves for 35 minutes and the rolls for 25 minutes or until the top of the bread is golden brown. Leave to cool in the tins for 15 minutes, then carefully turn the brioche out onto a wire rack to cool completely.

Best eaten within two days of baking, brioche can also be frozen for up to a month.

Genoise

This is possibly the most popular French cake. It is a classic whisked sponge enriched with a little butter. It can be used for layer cakes, roll cakes or even as the base of a mousse cake. The key to a successful Genoise is to be quick and light with the mixture. You need to fold in the flour very delicately, but in as few folds as possible. This is easiest to achieve by adding the flour in three additions and lightening the butter with a bit of the cake mix before folding together. As it has very little fat and is effectively a baked mousse, it is a great blank canvas and can be brushed with flavoured sugar syrups without making the cake soggy.

MAKES 1 × 23CM (9IN) CAKE

20g (¾oz) unsalted butter, melted and slightly cooled, plus extra for greasing
3 large eggs
80g (2¾oz) caster sugar
60g (2¼oz) plain flour
15g (½oz) cornflour

Preheat the oven to 180°C (160°C fan/350°F), Gas Mark 4 and lightly grease a deep 23cm (9in) cake tin, and line the base with baking parchment. Put the eggs and sugar in a large bowl and, using an electric whisk, beat for 5 minutes or until pale and thick, so that when the whisk is lifted from the bowl it forms a slowly dissolving ribbon that sits on the surface.

In a separate bowl, mix the flour and cornflour together and sift a third over the egg mixture, then very gently, fold together using a spatula. Repeat this process with the other two-thirds of flour mixture. Take a large spoonful of the egg mixture and add it to the butter, mixing them together until smooth. Tip this butter mixture back into the bowl with the egg mixture and carefully fold it in to combine.

Pour the sponge mixture into the prepared tin and spin the tin to level out the mixture. Bake for 20 minutes or until golden and coming away from the edges of the tin. Leave to cool for 10 minutes, then invert the cake onto a wire rack to cool completely.

JOCONDE ALMOND SPONGE

This is a moist almond sponge that is commonly used in layered cakes such as the classic Gâteau Opéra. It can be brushed with sugar syrups to add extra flavours, and you can use other nuts to give a different flavour and texture.

MAKES 2 × 33 × 23CM (13 × 9IN) LAYERS

25g (1oz) unsalted butter, melted, plus extra for greasing
3 large eggs
115g (4oz) ground almonds
115g (4oz) icing sugar
30g (1oz) plain flour
3 large egg whites
30g (1oz) caster sugar

Preheat the oven to 180°C (160°C fan/350°F), Gas 4 and grease two 33 × 23cm (13 × 9in) sheet pans and line with baking parchment, greasing the parchment too. Put the whole eggs, almonds and icing sugar in a large bowl and, using an electric whisk, beat together for 5 minutes or until pale and thick. Sift over the flour and fold together gently using a spatula. Drizzle over the melted butter and fold together to combine.

Put the egg whites in a clean, grease-free bowl and, using an electric mixer, whisk until foamy. Continue to whisk while you slowly pour in the sugar until the meringue holds soft peaks. Working in thirds, add the meringue to the egg mixture, folding together gently to combine. Divide the batter equally, by weight, between the two prepared tins, and very gently level it out. Bake for 8–10 minutes until light golden brown. Remove from the oven and immediately remove the sponges from the tins. Put them onto a wire rack to cool. While the sponges are still warm, trim off the edges, because they will crisp up slightly as they cool.

TIP

This base recipe can be used in a variety of different moulds and cake tins. The cooking time
will just need to be amended accordingly: the thinner the cake, the quicker the bake.

Meringue

To make meringue there are three basic methods: French, Italian and Swiss, and depending on the intended use, each has different pros and cons. French is the classic method made simply by whisking caster sugar into egg whites. Italian is the most technical: a sugar syrup is cooked to 118°C (244°F) and then poured into egg whites while whisking. Swiss is the method that falls between the two, with the sugar and egg whites cooked over a bain-marie before whisking to a glossy meringue. The benefit of Swiss- and Italian-style meringues is that they are cooked before baking, so they can be used to top recipes such as lemon tarts without being baked, giving a wonderful, almost marshmallow-like texture. For baked meringues, I prefer French or Swiss meringues, because the texture is often a little too chewy when made with Italian-style meringue. Swiss and Italian meringues also happen to be very flexible recipes, which can be turned into wonderful buttercreams. Whichever method you use, the ratio remains the same, one part egg white and two parts sugar, the most basic ratio in baking.

MAKES 12 SMALL MERINGUE NESTS OR 50 MINI MERINGUES

BASIC MERINGUE INGREDIENTS
3 large egg whites
240g (8½oz) caster sugar

FRENCH MERINGUE METHOD This is the easiest and best-known method, but it is also the least flexible, as it has to be baked before it can be eaten; however, it is still my choice for simple baked meringue recipes.

Put the egg whites and a pinch of cream of tartar or a few drops of lemon juice in a clean, grease-free bowl and, using an electric mixer, whisk on high speed until they form soft peaks. Continue to whisk while you slowly pour in the sugar until the meringue holds glossy peaks and is soft or stiff depending on the use.

SWISS MERINGUE METHOD This is my favourite method, because it combines the two other methods, giving a wonderful texture, and it is simple to make.

Put the egg whites and sugar in a large, grease-free heatproof bowl set over a pan of gently simmering water, making sure the base of the bowl doesn't touch the water. Whisk gently until the sugar has dissolved and the mixture is warm to the touch (you don't need to be vigorous here, you are simply heating the egg and sugar mixture together and preventing the whites from cooking).

To test the mixture is at the right temperature, simply dip two fingers into the bowl and rub them together, if you can still feel grains of sugar, the mixture isn't warm enough. If you are not baking this meringue and are worried about eating raw eggs, you can use an instant-read thermometer and cook the eggs until they reach 60°C (140°F), which will make it safe to eat.

Remove the bowl from the heat and, using an electric mixer, whisk on high speed until the meringue reaches the desired texture.

ITALIAN MERINGUE METHOD This method is the most precise and produces the most stable meringue, which is great used in more technical recipes.

Put 50ml (2fl oz) water and the caster sugar into a small pan set over a medium heat. Bring to the boil and have an instant-read thermometer ready. Meanwhile, put the egg whites in a clean, grease-free bowl (this is best done using a freestanding electric mixer). When the syrup in the pan reaches 115°C (239°F), start whisking the whites on high speed. Cook until the syrup registers 118°C (244°F), then remove from the heat and, with the mixer still running, slowly pour it into the meringue, avoiding the whisk. Once all the syrup has been added, whisk until the meringue holds the desired texture – this can take 5–10 minutes.

BAKING

Once the basic meringue has been made with your chosen method, all the meringue types are then baked in the same manner. Preheat the oven to 110°C (90°C fan/225°F), Gas Mark ¼ and line two baking trays with baking parchment. The meringue can either be spooned into small mounds or nest shapes, or into one large round (as if making a pavlova) or put into a piping bag fitted with a 1.5cm (⅝in) plain round piping tip and piped into shapes. They are then dried out in the preheated oven until crisp. Depending on the size, this can take between 1 and 2 hours. Once crisp, turn off the oven and allow the meringues to cool completely inside the oven. This helps the meringues to dry out completely.

TIPS

* Older egg whites whisk easier.

* Meringue needs a grease-free bowl, so it is best to avoid plastic bowls for mixing. Metal and glass bowls are preferable.

* You can rub the bowl with a cut lemon, then clean it with a piece of kitchen paper. This guarantees the bowl is free from grease and there is nothing to prevent the whites from whisking up.

* Always use egg whites at room temperature; cold whites will take longer to whisk.

* Don't stop midway through making a meringue. Stopping and starting can break down the meringue, resulting in a loss of volume.

* Avoid making meringues on a humid day, as it is harder to whisk to the desired texture and they will take longer to dry out in the oven.

Macarons

One of the most iconic French recipes, a macaron is a cookie that is made and sold around the world. It was, for a while, the 'it' pastry – the French cupcake – and it still rates as one of the most popular recipes. Below is a basic recipe to make the shell; try the praline buttercream (page 63), or the Earl Grey ganache (see page 122) as a filling. This recipe is a basic that can be used to decorate other recipes as well as making the little meringue cookies themselves.

MAKES 40

170g (6oz) icing sugar
160g (5¾oz) ground almonds
120ml (4fl oz) egg whites (from approx. 3 large eggs), divided into two equal batches
160g (5¾oz) caster sugar
1–2 teaspoons gel paste food colouring

Line two baking trays with baking parchment. Put the icing sugar and ground almonds in the bowl of a food processor and pulse about ten times until fully combined. (Or put in a bowl and stir well with a fork.) Sift this mixture into a large bowl, discarding any small particles that stay in the sieve. Add the first batch of egg whites to the almond mixture and mix together to form a thick paste, then set aside.

To make the meringue, put 50ml (2fl oz) water and the caster sugar in a small pan set over a medium-high heat. Bring to the boil, stirring occasionally, and cook until the syrup has dissolved. Once the syrup is clear and the sugar has dissolved, stop stirring and cook until the syrup registers 118°C (244°F) on an instant-read thermometer. Meanwhile, put the second batch of egg whites in a clean, grease-free bowl (this is best done using a freestanding electric mixer fitted with the whisk attachment). When the syrup reaches 115°C (239°F) on the thermometer, start whisking the whites on high speed until the meringue reaches soft peaks (once at this stage you shouldn't have to stop whisking – this wants to be a smooth motion, as the syrup should be at temperature). Once the syrup reaches 118°C (244°F), remove from the heat and pour it slowly down the side of the mixer bowl avoiding the whisk. Continue to whisk the meringue on high until the mixture has cooled slightly and the bowl is no longer hot to the touch but is still warm. Add the food colouring and whisk to combine. The meringue should be thick and glossy; if it is loose and looks wet, you either need to whisk a little longer or, most likely, your meringue wasn't whisked enough before adding the sugar syrup.

Scrape the meringue onto the almond mixture and mix together. If you lift the batter from the bowl it should fall in a thick ribbon from the spatula. This ribbon should fade back into the batter almost completely, leaving a faint trail behind. If the ribbon holds its shape on top of the batter, it needs a little more mixing. Transfer the batter to a piping bag fitted with a 1cm (½in) round piping tip. Pipe rounds about 2.5cm (1in) in diameter onto the prepared baking trays. Leave to rest for 30 minutes or until the macarons have developed a skin and are no longer sticky. Preheat the oven to 180°C (160°C fan/350°F), Gas Mark 4.

Bake for 12 minutes or until you can lightly tap the macarons and they feel firm; if they feel very delicate they need a few more minutes of baking. Remove the trays from the oven and slide the parchment onto the work surface and leave the macarons to cool for a few minutes before gently peeling them off the paper. The macarons will keep for up to a week in the refrigerator, but frozen they will keep perfectly for two months.

Biscuits à La Cuillère
(Sponge Fingers)

Depending on where in the world you live, this recipe goes by the name of 'sponge fingers', 'lady fingers' and, of course, the French name, 'biscuits à la cuillère'. A very simple mixture of meringue, egg yolks and flour is transformed into a light sponge finger that is used to make the classic recipe, the Charlotte (see page 68), but it can also be used in trifles and even in Italian tiramisu.

MAKES ABOUT 50

3 large eggs, separated
100g (3½oz) caster sugar
75g (2½oz) plain flour
2 tablespoons icing sugar

Preheat the oven to 180°C (160°C fan/350°F), Gas Mark 4 and line two baking trays with baking parchment. Put the egg whites in a clean, grease-free bowl and, using an electric mixer, whisk until they form soft peaks. Continue to whisk while you slowly pour in the sugar until the meringue holds stiff and glossy peaks.

Beat the egg yolks in a separate bowl until pale and thickened, then scrape them onto the meringue and carefully fold together using a spatula. In two additions, sift the flour over the meringue and gently fold together, trying to keep the mixture as light as possible. Transfer the mixture to a piping bag fitted with a 1.5cm (⅝in) plain round piping tip.

Pipe the mixture onto the prepared baking trays, creating fingers about 10cm (4in) long. Dust the fingers with the icing sugar and then bake for 10–12 minutes or until golden. Remove the trays from the oven and allow the fingers to cool on the trays to room temperature.

You can use the fingers immediately or they can be wrapped well and frozen for up to one month.

TIP
Although the recipe is traditionally used to make sponge fingers, as above, you can also spread this batter into a thin layer and bake it to make thin sheets of sponge that can be used in a similar way to the joconde recipe (see page 172).

Crème Pâtissière

Pastry cream is an alternative name for crème pâtissière, a custard that has been thickened with either flour or cornflour and is used in a wide variety of recipes, including éclairs and fruit tarts. It's one of the true building blocks of French baking.

MAKES 800G (1LB 12OZ)

1 vanilla pod or 2 teaspoons
  vanilla bean paste
500ml (18fl oz) whole milk
2 large eggs
4 egg yolks
200g (7oz) caster sugar
50g (1¾oz) cornflour

Cut the vanilla pod, if using, in half and scrape out the seeds. Put the seeds or vanilla bean paste in a large pan and pour in the milk. Put over a medium-high heat and bring to the boil.

Meanwhile, put the eggs and yolks in a heatproof bowl and add the sugar and cornflour, then whisk until smooth. Pour the boiling milk over, whisking constantly to combine. Pour this mixture into the pan, return to a medium heat, and whisk constantly until thickened, cooking for a few minutes extra to remove the taste of the cornflour.

Pour this custard into a clean bowl and add any additional flavourings, such as praline paste or orange blossom water to taste. Press a piece of clingfilm onto the surface of the custard, then put it in the refrigerator until needed.

The covered pastry cream will keep for up to three days in the refrigerator.

Crème Mousseline

Somewhere between a thickened custard and a buttercream, crème mousseline is simply a crème pâtissière with added butter. It is commonly used as a filling and is probably best known as the filling for the classic Fraisier (see page 59).

MAKES 1.5KG (3LB 5OZ)

1 vanilla pod or 2 teaspoons
  vanilla bean paste
500ml (18fl oz) whole milk
2 large eggs
4 egg yolks
200g (7oz) caster sugar
75g (2½oz) cornflour
250g (9oz) unsalted butter, diced

Cut the vanilla pod, if using, in half and scrape out the seeds. Put the seeds or vanilla bean paste in a large pan and add the milk. Bring to the boil over a medium-high heat.

Meanwhile, put the eggs and yolks in a heatproof bowl and add the sugar and cornflour, then whisk until smooth. Pour the boiling milk over, whisking constantly to combine. Pour this mixture back into the pan, return to a medium heat, and whisk constantly until thickened, cooking for a few minutes extra to remove the taste of the cornflour.

Pour this mixture into a clean bowl and add half the butter, stirring until melted and combined. Press a piece of clingfilm onto the surface of the custard and put it in the refrigerator for a few hours until the crème is fully chilled.

To finish the mousseline, put the remaining butter in the bowl of an electric mixer and beat together until pale and creamy. Add the mousseline in four additions, beating until the butter is fully incorporated. This can now be used as you wish, as a cake or pastry filling.

This will keep for up to three days in the refrigerator. Bring to room temperature before using and beat until smooth, then use according to the recipe.

TIP
This can be flavoured in many different ways. If making the Fraisier (see page 59), for example, I simply add 2 teaspoons of kirsch, with the first portion of butter, but you can also use nut pastes and pralines and, of course, melted and slightly cooled chocolate.

Buttercream

Obviously, I couldn't write a book on baking and not cover buttercream, but instead of using the overly sweet classic buttercream I grew up with – made simply with butter and icing sugar – I want to introduce you to what I think of as 'real' buttercream. Both of the recipes here are based on a cooked egg mixture, either with egg whites or egg yolks. (You can also use a combination of the two, see page 63.) This provides buttercreams with wonderful smooth and silky textures.

The first buttercream is known as Swiss meringue buttercream, because it uses the Swiss meringue technique, where egg whites and sugar are whisked over a bain-marie until warm and then whisked, off the heat, until a wonderfully glossy meringue is formed. There is another recipe very similar in finish called Italian meringue buttercream, which instead of cooking over a bain-marie uses a hot sugar syrup (as in the Macarons recipe on page 176) but for the purposes of this book, I have stuck to the Swiss version, as I find it a lot easier and more straightforward.

The second recipe is known as French buttercream and uses egg yolks as its base. This gives the buttercream a rich finish that doesn't quite hold its shape as well as the Swiss version but is perfect as a filling for macarons and cakes. Both styles of buttercream can be flavoured easily with melted and cooled chocolate, fruit purées or even nut pastes.

MAKES 750G (1LB 10OZ)

3 large egg whites
250g (9oz) caster sugar
375g (13oz) unsalted butter, at room
  temperature, diced

FOR THE SWISS MERINGUE BUTTERCREAM

Put the egg whites and sugar in a large, grease-free, heatproof bowl and set over a pan of gently simmering water, making sure the base of the bowl doesn't touch the water. Lightly whisk this mixture until the sugar has dissolved and it is hot to the touch (you aren't trying to form the meringue at this stage, you just want to keep the mixture moving so that the whites don't cook). To test this, you could check the mixture has come to about 60°C (140°F) on an instant-read thermometer or, more simply, dip your fingers into the whites and rub them together; if you can't feel any sugar grains, the mixture is hot enough.

Remove the bowl from the heat and, using an electric mixer, whisk for 7–8 minutes until the meringue is thick and glossy and the mixture has returned to room temperature. Once cooled, slowly add the butter, a couple of pieces at a time, beating until you have a smooth, silky buttercream. If at any point the buttercream looks soupy or curdled, don't worry – keep mixing and adding the butter. It should come back together, but if after adding all the butter it still looks curdled, simply keep whisking, eventually it will smooth out (see photo opposite).

At this stage the buttercream can be flavoured, either simply with some vanilla bean paste or with whatever you want – chocolate, pistachio paste or even lemon curd. Flavour it in the exactly the same way as you would any buttercream recipe.

MAKES 350G (12OZ)

100g (3½oz) caster sugar
3 large egg yolks
225g (8oz) unsalted butter, at room
  temperature, diced

TIP
Although both recipes do
cook the egg yolks or whites
using a bain-marie or a
hot sugar syrup, if you are
concerned about eating
unpasteurized egg you can
also use pasteurized egg
whites or yolks, which are
becoming more common in
supermarkets (look in the
chilled aisles). Just bear in
mind that they don't always
whip up quite as well.

FOR THE FRENCH MERINGUE BUTTERCREAM

Put the sugar and 2 tablespoons of water in a small pan over a medium-high heat and cook, without stirring, until the sugar syrup reaches 120°C (248°F) on an instant-read thermometer. Meanwhile, put the egg yolks in the bowl of an electric mixer fitted with the whisk attachment and whisk on high speed until the yolks are pale and have thickened (this is best done using a freestanding electric mixer). When the whisk is lifted from the bowl, the yolks should form a thick ribbon. When the syrup is at temperature, remove the pan from the heat and, while whisking constantly, carefully pour the syrup into the yolk mixture, avoiding the whisk.

Continue to whisk until the yolk mixture (also known as pâte à bombe) has cooled to room temperature and is thick and light. Once cooled, slowly add the butter, a couple of pieces at a time, beating until you have a smooth and silky buttercream. As with the recipe opposite, this can be flavoured as you wish, according to the specific recipe.

Both buttercreams will keep for up to a week in the refrigerator. Bring to room temperature and beat until light and fluffy before using.

Caramelized White Chocolate

For some people, white chocolate is too sweet and has little taste, but this method of caramelizing the chocolate gives it an amazing flavour, with notes of dulce de leche and caramel – wonderful stuff! It can be used in all recipes where white chocolate is used, giving the recipe a different dimension and a more interesting flavour.

MAKES 300G (10½OZ)

300g (10½oz) good-quality white chocolate (minimum 30 per cent cocoa butter), roughly chopped

Preheat the oven to 120°C (100°C fan/250°F), Gas Mark ½. Put the chocolate on a non-stick baking tray, and bake for 10 minutes. Remove the tray from the oven and give the chocolate a really good stir.

Return to the oven and repeat this process over the space of 1 hour or until the chocolate is a wonderful caramel colour. As you go through this process, the chocolate will change in appearance – sometimes smooth and glossy, sometimes thick and grainy – but don't worry, keep stirring and cooking, and it will smooth out. Once fully caramelized, pour the chocolate into a clean, sterilized jar. Stored in a sealed jar and kept in a cool place, the chocolate will keep for a couple of months.

When you are ready to use the chocolate, put the jar in a pan of warm water until the chocolate has melted, then pour it from the jar, using it according to the specific recipe.

TIP
The higher the cocoa butter content, the easier this method seems to work, so don't use cheap white chocolate – this is the time to use good quality.

Crème Chantilly

This is the simplest of recipes, but it can turn a bowl of fresh berries into a wonderful and quick dessert. The key to Chantilly is to whip the cream only to soft peaks. If you go too far, the texture will be too firm and can become grainy. It's always better to err on the side of caution.

MAKES 300ML (½ PINT)

300ml (½ pint) whipping cream
1 tablespoon caster sugar
1 teaspoon vanilla extract

Put the cream, sugar and vanilla in a large cold bowl (I prefer metal) and, using either an electric whisk or a traditional balloon whisk, whisk until the cream is just starting to hold soft peaks.

You can use the cream immediately or it can be covered and transferred to the refrigerator until needed. Bear in mind that if the cream is chilled it will firm up further as it chills; it is best served immediately.

Crème Anglaise

Crème anglaise is the basic French custard. It is used in all manner of desserts, and is delicious both warm and cold. The key to a creamy custard is very gentle cooking – if cooked over too high a heat you risk scrambling the mixture. I like to use an instant-read thermometer to check the temperature, which should be 75–80°C (167–176°F). This tells you that the eggs have fully cooked and the custard will have the correct texture.

MAKES 650ML (22FL OZ)

1 vanilla pod or 2 teaspoons
  vanilla bean paste
400ml (14fl oz) whole milk
100ml (3½fl oz) whipping cream
5 large egg yolks
80g (2¾oz) caster sugar

Cut the vanilla pod, if using, in half and scrape out the seeds. Put the seeds and pod, or the vanilla bean paste, in a large pan and add the milk and cream. Bring to the boil over a medium heat.

Meanwhile, whisk the egg yolks and the sugar together in a heatproof bowl until the sugar has dissolved and the mixture is pale and thick. Take out and discard the vanilla pod (or wash and dry it and use it to flavour a jar of sugar). Continue to whisk the yolks constantly as you slowly pour the boiling milk over them.

Pour this custard back into the pan and cook over a medium heat, stirring constantly using a wooden spoon, until the custard thickens enough to coat the back of the spoon (or until it reaches 75–80°C/167–176°F on an instant-read thermometer). Pour the custard through a fine sieve into a clean bowl. Use immediately or press a sheet of clingfilm onto the surface of the custard and put it in the refrigerator until needed.

The covered crème anglaise will keep for up to three days in the refrigerator.

TIP
This also makes a wonderful ice cream. Churn the custard in an ice cream maker after it has chilled in the refrigerator overnight.

Praline and Nut Pastes

These are one of my favourite ways to add flavour to a recipe. They can be folded into a mousse or added to buttercream, and they give a wonderfully rich flavour. They are super-easy to prepare, and making them at home saves you a lot of money, because store-bought versions can be very expensive. The difference between praline paste and a simple nut paste is the amount of sugar they contain. Praline generally has equal parts sugar to nuts, giving a sweet, caramelized flavour, whereas nut pastes have very little or no sugar (I add a small amount of sugar as it helps the nuts to break down).

TIP

The type of nuts are given as examples, but you can adapt them to your preferences, the praline can be made with all nuts, either on their own or in combination.

FOR THE PRALINE PASTE

150g (5½oz) blanched hazelnuts
150g (5½oz) caster sugar
pinch of flaked sea salt

Preheat the oven to 180°C (160°C fan/350°F), Gas Mark 4 and line a baking tray with baking parchment. Put the nuts on the tray and bake for 10–15 minutes until browned and fragrant. Remove the tray from the oven and set aside while you cook the sugar.

Put the sugar in a small pan over a medium heat, and cook, without stirring, until the sugar has dissolved and is a dark amber brown. (Be careful that it doesn't cook too far as it can burn easily.) Remove the pan from the heat and pour the caramel over the nuts, then leave to set.

Break into chunks and put them in the bowl of a food processor. Pulse until the chunks are broken down a little, then process until smooth. With a domestic processor this can take a while, the mixture will first look powdery, but with enough time the nuts will break down and release their oils, making a smooth paste. Add the salt and process to combine.

When making praline pastes, the food processor or blender will be on for a long time. If you are worried about the machine overheating, stop for 10 minutes before continuing.

FOR THE PISTACHIO PASTE

200g (7oz) blanched pistachio nuts
2 tablespoons caster sugar

Preheat the oven to 180°C (160°C fan/350°F), Gas Mark 4 and line a baking tray with baking parchment. Put the nuts on the tray and bake for 10 minutes or until lightly toasted and fragrant.

Remove from the oven and tip into the bowl of a food processor along with the sugar. Process until smooth. With domestic food processors this can take about 10 minutes, so be careful your machine doesn't overheat. If you feel the machine is getting too hot, allow it to cool down for 10 minutes before continuing.

Both of the above recipes can be stored in a sterilized jar in the refrigerator for up to a month.

Salted Caramel Sauce

In my house, this recipe gets made a lot. I use it as a sauce for ice cream, to serve with crêpes and even as a filling for brownies. It has a wonderful, rich caramel flavour that comes from properly cooking the sugar and caramelizing it to a deep copper brown.

MAKES 275ML (9½FL OZ)

150g (5½oz) caster sugar
¼ teaspoon flaked sea salt
120ml (4fl oz) whipping cream
10g (¼oz) unsalted butter

Put the sugar in a medium pan over a medium heat. Cook, without stirring, until the sugar starts to caramelize around the outside of the pan.

Meanwhile, put the salt, cream and butter in a small pan over a medium heat to warm through.

Using a heatproof spatula or a wooden spoon, carefully draw the caramelized sugar towards the centre of the pan, to help the sugar cook evenly. Once all the sugar has caramelized to a rich golden brown, remove from the heat and carefully add half the cream – this will bubble up violently, so pour slowly. Once the bubbling has settled, add the remaining cream and cook until smooth. If, after adding the cream, you have lumps of caramel, return the pan to a medium-low heat and cook until the lumps have dissolved and the caramel is smooth. Pour the caramel into a jug and use as a sauce or a filling, depending on the recipe. Kept in a sealed container in the refrigerator, the sauce will keep for up to two weeks.

TIP
The above recipe gives a general-purpose consistency that is thick but still pourable at room temperature. You can adjust the texture of the caramel by changing the amount of cream: more if you want a thinner, more pourable sauce, or less if you want a thicker caramel.

Tempering Chocolate

Learning how to temper chocolate is an important technique because it enables you to use chocolate in different ways – ways that simply melting it won't achieve. Tempering is basically a way of melting and cooling the chocolate so that when it sets it crystallizes in such a way that it is stable. It gives the chocolate a shine, it won't melt when handled and it has a great snap to it.

By tempering the chocolate, it can be used to make chocolate decorations and to make your own chocolate bars and truffles. It also means that whatever you have made with the chocolate doesn't need to be kept in the refrigerator. If you coated truffles in melted chocolate, it wouldn't set properly at room temperature and would become tacky, so it has to be chilled. It would also melt at the lightest touch. This might seem like a mysterious technique, as it doesn't look as if much is changing, but it is a fairly simple and straightforward process, as long as you follow the temperatures carefully.

MAKES 300G (10½OZ)

300g (10½oz) dark, milk or white chocolate, roughly chopped

Put three-quarters of the chocolate in a heatproof bowl set over a pan of gently simmering water, making sure the base of the bowl doesn't touch the water. By keeping the water at a very low simmer the chocolate melts slowly, which makes it easier to temper.

Using a probe instant-read thermometer, melt the chocolate slowly, stirring regularly, until it reaches 50–55°C (122–131°F) for dark chocolate or 45°C (113°F) for milk and white chocolate. Remove the bowl from the heat and add the remaining chocolate, stirring constantly until the chocolate has melted and it has lowered in temperature to 28–29°C (82–84°F) for dark chocolate or 27–28°C (81–82°F) for milk and white chocolate.

Return the bowl to the heat and, stirring constantly, heat it up for 1 minute or until the temperature of the chocolate has increased to 31–32°C (88–90°F) for dark chocolate or 28–29°C (82–84°F) for milk and white chocolate – this is what is known as the chocolate's 'working temperature'.

The chocolate should now be tempered. To test, dip a knife into the chocolate and allow the excess to drip off and set onto a piece of baking parchment. If, after 2 minutes, it has set with no streaks showing, the chocolate has successfully been tempered; if it is streaky, you will need to start again.

TIP
The chocolate you start with needs to be tempered itself, so make sure you are using good-quality chocolate that has been stored in a cool place. If it is streaky when you take it out of the packet, it has been kept poorly and won't temper very well using the above method.

If, as you dip truffles into the chocolate or make decorations with it, the chocolate starts to thicken and cool, return the bowl to the heat to bring it back to its working temperature, making sure it doesn't get any hotter, or you will have to start again.

Resources

www.chefs.net
General bakeware and specialist equipment, including tart rings and Saint Honoré piping tubes

www.divertimenti.co.uk
www.lakeland.co.uk
General bakeware and disposable piping bags

www.kitchenaid.co.uk
Freestanding electric mixers, food processors, electric hand mixers

www.teapigs.co.uk
Matcha powder: the Japanese fine green tea powder

www.souschef.co.uk
Black sesame powder, edible gold leaf, freeze-dried fruit powder, cacao nibs, vanilla pods, tonka beans, pearl sugar

www.natcofoods.com
Rose syrup

www.kingsfinefood.co.uk
Amedei chocolate

www.chocolate.co.uk
Valrhona chocolate

www.waitrose.com
Valrhona and Green & Black's cocoa powder

www.hbingredients.co.uk
Cacao Barry chocolate

www.almondart.com
Pouring fondant

PÂTISSERIES IN FRANCE

This list is far from comprehensive, but it includes some of the many pâtisseries that I have visited and loved over the last few years of travelling around France. The list doesn't include the many pâtisseries I have visited in smaller towns and villages, as often these were stumbled upon and no website or details could be found later on, but, as the cliché goes, every town in France seems to have a good pâtisserie, and sometimes the fun is in just unexpectedly finding one of these little hidden gems.

PARIS

Pierre Hermé, 72 rue Bonaparte, 75006 Paris
www.pierreherme.com

Un Dimanche à Paris, 4–8 Cour du Commerce Saint André, 75006 Paris
www.un-dimanche-a-paris.com

L'Éclair de Génie, 14 rue Pavée, 75004 Paris
www.leclairdegenie.com

Jacques Genin, 133 rue de Turenne, 75003 Paris
www.jacquesgenin.fr

Ladurée, 16–18 rue Royale, 75008 Paris
www.laduree.com

LYON

Bouillet, 15 Place de la Croix-Rousse, 69004 Lyon
www.chocolatier-bouillet.com

Bernachon, 42 cours Franklin Roosevelt, 69006 Lyon
www.bernachon.com

Délices des Sens, 12 boulevard des Brotteaux, 69006 Lyon
www.chocolat-delices-des-sens.com

Sève, 29 quai Saint-Antoine, 69002 Lyon
www.chocolatseve.com

NORTH-WEST FRANCE
Christophe Roussel, 19 avenue de Gaulle, 44500 La Baule
www.christophe-roussel.fr

Pâtisserie Dupont, 42 rue Gaston Manneville, 14160 Dives-Sur-Mer
www.dupontavecunthe.fr

NORTH-EAST FRANCE
Pâtisserie Christian, 12 rue de l'Outre, 67000 Strasbourg
www.christian.fr

Pâtisserie Vincent Dallet, 47 cours Jean-Baptiste Langlet, 51100 Reims
www.chocolat-vincentdallet.fr

SOUTH-WEST FRANCE
Henriet, place Georges Clemenceau, 64200 Biarritz
www.chocolaterie-henriet.com

Macarons de Saint-Émilion, 9 rue Guadet, 33330 Saint-Émilion
www.macarons-saint-emilion.fr

SOUTH-EAST FRANCE
Pâtisserie Intuitions, 22 rue Bivouac Napoléon, 06400 Cannes
www.patisserie-intuitions.com

Pâtisserie Lac, 18 rue Barla, 06000 Nice
www.patisseries-lac.com

Index

A

almonds: almond Bostock 64
  almond croissants 44
  fig and star anise tart 26
  financiers 98
  galette des rois 49
  gâteau opéra 132–134
  joconde almond sponge 172
  macaron à l'ancienne 111
  macarons 176
  pear tart 23
  Amaretto and peach baba 70
apples: apple compote 77
  apple turnovers 41
  simple apple tart 40
apricot Danish 48

B

baba, Amaretto and peach 70
banana tarte tatin 65
bavarois: caramelized white chocolate
  146–148
  raspberry 70
beeswax: canelés 96
biscuits: chocolate sablés 106
  macaron à l'ancienne 111
  macarons 176
  sablés Breton 104
  vanilla sablés 105
biscuits à la cuillère 177
  coffee tart 24
  mixed berry charlotte 68
blackcurrants: cassis religieuse 37
blood-orange marshmallows 127
blueberries: breakfast brioche buns 100
breakfast brioche buns 100
brioche 170
  almond Bostock 64
  breakfast brioche buns 100
  brioche Suisse 99
  tarte Tropezienne 103
bûche de Noël 65–66
buns: breakfast brioche buns 100
  coconut and strawberry choux buns 33
  salambos 27
butter 11
buttercream 180–181
  coffee 132–4
  French meringue 179
  French sesame seed 135–138
  praline 65–66
  rose 130
  Swiss meringue 178
  tonka bean 151

C

cakes: canelés 96
  cherry and almond financiers 98
  concorde 152
  fraisier 59–60
  gâteau au chocolat 53–54
  gâteau Breton 67
  gâteau opéra 132–134
  Genoise 172–173
  joconde almond sponge 172
  kougelhopf 108
  lemon madeleines 94
  lemon pound cake 56
  matcha, black sesame and white
    chocolate cake 135–138
  rose, raspberry and lychee cake 130
candied peel 118
canelés 96
caramel: banana tarte tatin 65
  canelés 96
  caramelized pears 146–148
  caramelized pineapple crêpes 89
  caramelized white chocolate 182
  caramelized white chocolate, ginger
    caramel and macadamia tarts 146–148
  caramels 121
  chocolate, caramel and hazelnut
    tarts 145
  chocolate soufflé tarts with
    salted caramel 19
  crème brûlée 82
  crème caramel 81
  croquembouche 142–144
  gâteau St Honoré 139–140
  île flottantes 86
  kouign amann 42–44
  milk chocolate and hazelnut
    praline bûche de Noël 63–64
  millefeuille 38
  praline 184
  salambos 27
  salted caramel sauce 185
  speculoos and milk chocolate
    éclairs 35
cassis religieuse 37
chai tea caramels 121
Chantilly cream *see* crème Chantilly
charlotte, mixed berry 68
cherries: cherry and almond
  financiers 98
  clafoutis 76
  pistachio and cherry soufflés 75
chestnuts: Mont Blanc 84
chocolate 11
  brioche Suisse 99
caramelized white chocolate 182
caramelized white chocolate,
  ginger caramel and macadamia
    tarts 146–148
chocolate, caramel and hazelnut
    tarts 145
chocolate fondants 72
chocolate mousse 83
chocolate sablés 106
chocolate soufflé tarts with
    salted caramel 19
chocolate tart 151
coffee and white chocolate coffee 24
concorde 152
Earl Grey truffles 122
éclairs 35
ganache 20
gâteau au chocolat 53–54
gâteau opéra 132–134
glaze 55–6
hot chocolate sauce 90
matcha, black sesame and
  white chocolate cake 135–138
milk chocolate and hazelnut
    praline bûche de Noël 63–64
orangettes 118
palet d'or 123
passion fruit and chocolate tart 20
pavé au chocolat 125
sweet chocolate pastry 158–160
tempering 186–187
chouquettes 114
choux pastry 156-7
  cassis religieuse 37
  chouquettes 114
  coconut and strawberry choux buns 33
  croquembouche 142–144
  éclairs 35
  gâteau St Honoré 139–140
  Paris-Brest 30
  salambos 27
clafoutis 76
coconut and strawberry choux buns 33
coffee: coffee tart 24
  gâteau opéra 132–134
concorde 152
confectionery: blood-orange
  marshmallows 127
  caramels 121
  Earl Grey truffles 122
  orangettes 118
  palet d'or 123
  pâte de fruit 117
  pavé au chocolat 125
craquelin: cassis religieuse 37

cream 11
caramels 121
chocolate Chantilly 145
coffee and white chocolate coffee 24
crème brûlée 82
crème Chantilly 139–140, 183
Earl Grey truffles 122
ganache 20
gâteau au chocolat 53–54
mascarpone cream 24
Mont Blanc 84
palet d'or 123
pavé au chocolat 125
tarte Tropezienne 103
white chocolate mousse 152
crème anglaise 183
île flottantes 86
crème brûlée 82
crème caramel 81
crème Chantilly 183
chocolate Chantilly 145
gâteau St Honoré 139–140
crème légère: millefeuille 38
tarte Tropezienne 103
crème mousseline 179
fraisier 59–60
Paris-Brest 30
crème pâtissière 178
apricot Danish 48
breakfast brioche buns 100
brioche Suisse 99
cassis religieuse 37
coconut and strawberry choux buns 33
crème mousseline 179
croquembouche 142–144
flan Parisien 28
gâteau St Honoré 139–140
raspberry tarts 14
salambos 27
tarte Tropezienne 103
crêpes, caramelized pineapple 89
croissant dough 166–168
almond croissants 44
apricot Danish 48
croissants 166
kouign amann 42–44
pain au raisin 47
croquembouche 142–144
custard: breakfast brioche buns 100
brioche Suisse 99
clafoutis 76
crème anglaise 183
crème brûlée 82
crème caramel 81
crème pâtissière 178

far Breton 78
flan Parisien 28
île flottantes 86

D

Danish, apricot 48

E

Earl Grey truffles 122
éclairs 35
eggs 11
meringues 174–175
equipment 8–9

F

far Breton 78
fig and star anise tart 26
financiers 98
flan Parisien 28
fondants, chocolate 72
fraisier 59–60
frangipane: almond Bostock 64
fig and star anise tart 26
galette des rois 49
pear tart 23
French buttercream 135–138
French meringue buttercream 181
fruit 11

G

galette des rois 49
ganache 20, 132–134
coffee and white chocolate coffee 24
Earl Grey truffles 122
palet d'or 123
gâteau au chocolat 55–56
gâteau Breton 67
gâteau opéra 132–134
gâteau St Honoré 139–140
Genoise 61–62, 130, 172–173
ginger: caramelized white chocolate, ginger caramel and macadamia tarts 146–148
glazes: caramelized white chocolate 146–148
chocolate 55–56, 132–134, 135–138
lemon 58, 94

H

hazelnuts: chocolate, caramel and hazelnut tarts 145
milk chocolate and hazelnut praline bûche de Noël 63–64
Paris-Brest 30
praline 184

I

île flottantes 86

J

joconde almond sponge 132–134, 172
matcha joconde sponge 135–138

K

kougelhopf 108
kouign amann 42–44

L

lemon: lemon madeleines 94
lemon pound cake 56
lemon syrup 61–62
lemon tart 16
lining tart tins 164–165
lychees: rose, raspberry and lychee cake 130

M

macadamia nuts: caramelized white chocolate, ginger caramel and macadamia tarts 146–148
macarons 176
macaron à l'ancienne 111
rose, raspberry and lychee cake 130
madeleines, lemon 94
mangos: pâte de fruit 117
marshmallows, blood-orange 127
marzipan: fraisier 59–60
mascarpone cream 24
matcha, black sesame and white chocolate cake 135–138
meringues 174–175
concorde 152
île flottantes 86
milk chocolate and hazelnut praline bûche de Noël 63–64
millefeuille 38
Mont Blanc 84
mousses: chocolate 83
white chocolate 152

O

oranges: blood-orange marshmallows 127
caramelized pineapple crêpes 89
orangettes 118

P

pain au raisin 47
palet d'or 123
palmiers 112
Paris-Brest 30
passion fruit: passion fruit and

chocolate tart 20
passion fruit and milk
    chocolate éclairs 35
passion fruit caramels 121
pastes: pistachio 184
    praline 184
pastries: almond croissants 44
    apple turnovers 41
    apricot Danish 48
    cassis religieuse 37
    chouquettes 114
    croquembouche 142–144
    éclairs 35
    galette des rois 49
    gâteau St Honoré 139–140
    kouign amann 42–44
    millefeuille 38
    pain au raisin 47
    palmiers 112
    Paris-Brest 30
    salambos 27
    see also tarts
pastry 13–49
    lining tart tins 164–165
    pâte à choux (choux pastry) 156–157
    pâte brisée (shortcrust pastry) 160
    pâte sucrée (sweet pastry) 158–160
    rough puff pastry 162–163
    sweet chocolate pastry 158–160
pastry cream *see* crème pâtissière
pâte à choux (choux pastry) 156–157
pâte brisée (shortcrust pastry) 160
pâte de fruit 117
pâte sucrée (sweet pastry) 158–160
pavé au chocolat 125
peaches: Amaretto and peach baba 70
pears: caramelized pears 146–148
    pear tart 23
peel, candied 118
pineapple: caramelized pineapple
    crêpes 89
    concorde 152
pistachio nuts: apricot Danish 48
    pistachio and cherry soufflés 75
    pistachio paste 184
pound cake, lemon 58
praline 184
    milk chocolate and hazelnut
        praline bûche de Noël 63–64
prunes: far Breton 78
    gâteau Breton 67
puff pastry 162–3
    apple turnovers 41
    banana tarte tatin 65
    galette des rois 49
    gâteau St Honoré 139–140

millefeuille 38
palmiers 112
simple apple tart 40

R

raisins: galette des rois 49
    pain au raisin 47
raspberries: mixed berry charlotte 68
    pâte de fruit 117
    raspberry tarts 14
    rose, raspberry and lychee cake 130
religieuse, cassis 37
rice pudding 77
rose, raspberry and lychee cake 130
rough puff pastry 162–163
rum: banana tarte tatin 65
    canelés 96
    galette des rois 49

S

sablés: chocolate 106
    sablés Breton 104
    vanilla 105
salambos 27
salt 11
salted caramel: salted butter
    caramels 121
    chocolate soufflé tarts with salted
        caramel 19
    salted caramel sauce 185
sauces: crème anglaise 183
    hot chocolate sauce 90
    salted caramel sauce 185
sesame seeds: matcha, black sesame
    and white chocolate cake 135–138
shortcrust pastry 160
soufflés, pistachio and cherry 75
speculoos and milk chocolate éclairs 35
sponge: chocolate 65–66
    Genoise 61–62, 130, 172–173
    joconde almond 132–134, 172
    matcha joconde 135–138
sponge fingers *see* biscuits à la cuillère
star anise: fig and star anise tart 26
strawberries: coconut and strawberry
choux buns 33
    fraisier 59–60
sugar 11
sweet pastry 158–160
Swiss meringue buttercream 180

T

tart tins, lining 164–165
tarte Tropezienne 103
tarts: banana tarte tatin 65

caramelized white chocolate, ginger
    caramel and macadamia tarts 146–148
chocolate, caramel and hazelnut
    tarts 145
chocolate soufflé tarts with
    salted caramel 19
chocolate tart 151
coffee tart 24
fig and star anise tart 26
lemon tart 16
passion fruit and chocolate tart 20
pear tart 23
raspberry tarts 14
simple apple tart 40
tea: chai tea caramels 121
    Earl Grey truffles 122
    matcha, black sesame and white
        chocolate cake 135–138
tempering chocolate 186–187
tonka bean buttercream 151
truffles: Earl Grey truffles 122
    palet d'or 123
    pavé au chocolat 125
turnovers, apple 41

V

vanilla 11
    vanilla sablés 105

W

waffles 90

Y

yeast: brioche 170
    croissant dough 166–168

Acknowledgements

I really should start by thanking my parents who, when we were little, took my brother and me on many trips to France. You encouraged us to speak French and to always be willing to try something new. These trips have stayed with me all these years and I can see their influence throughout this book.

Writing, for me, always starts off as a solitary affair. I spend months locked away in my kitchen, endlessly testing and retesting recipes. During these months I have a very strong idea of how the book is going to look but it is only once this stage is finished that the book really starts to come to life, when a team of brilliant, funny and amazingly creative people jump on board and help turn my recipes into the beautiful book you have in your hands.

A huge thanks to Laura, Tabitha and Joss because working with you has been an absolute joy, can I have you on every shoot please? The images in this book are stunning and that is all down to the three of you. Thanks to Rachel, Kathryn and Jenna for helping keep our manic days on track and in order. Helen, it is always great when a designer seems to be on the same wavelength and you have designed the book I wanted; it is beautiful, thank you. Vicky, you have been a brilliant editor and I have always felt in very safe hands, thank you so much.

To Kyle and the whole team at Kyle Books, for giving me another opportunity to write for them, I am so thankful, and so proud of the book that we have produced.

Thanks to Matt and Simon for letting me take over your kitchens, I hope the cakes made up for it! Thanks to everyone I force-fed cake during testing, I know it wasn't exactly a chore but your feedback is always appreciated.

Thanks to Kat for looking after me, working with you always feels like a collaboration and you get what I am aiming for.

Of course my biggest thanks has to go to you for buying this book; I write these books because I want to get you in the kitchen baking, when you share pictures of your cakes it makes me really happy to see the recipe come to life, so please keep them coming!

THANKS EDD X

FSC — MIX
Paper | Supporting responsible forestry
www.fsc.org FSC® C008047

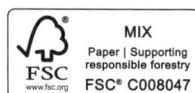

First published in Great Britain in 2014 by Kyle Books an imprint of Octopus Publishing Group Ltd
Carmelite House
50 Victoria Embankment
London EC4Y 0DZ
www.octopusbooks.co.uk

An Hachette UK Company
www.hachette.co.uk

The authorised representative in the EEA is Hachette Ireland, 8 Castlecourt Centre, Castleknock Road, Castleknock, Dublin 15, D15 YF6A, Ireland (email: info@hbgi.ie)

This edition published in 2025

This material was previously published as *Patisserie Made Simple*

Text © Edd Kimber 2014, 2025
Photographs © Laura Edwards
Design © Octopus Publishing Group 2014, 2025

Distributed in the US by Hachette Book Group
1290 Avenue of the Americas, 4th and 5th Floors, New York, NY 10104

Distributed in Canada by Canadian Manda Group
664 Annette St., Toronto, Ontario, Canada M6S 2C8

ISBN 978 1 80419 315 0

A CIP catalogue record for this title is available from the British Library

Printed and bound in China

10 9 8 7 6 5 4 3 2 1

Editor: Vicky Orchard
Photographer: Laura Edwards
Food stylist: Joss Herd
Props stylist: Tabitha Hawkins
Production: Lucy Carter and Nic Jones